THE ERRAND OF FORM

THE
ERRAND OF FORM
AN ASSAY OF
JANE AUSTEN'S ART

JOSEPH WIESENFARTH, F.S.C.

FORDHAM UNIVERSITY PRESS
NEW YORK   1967

Printed in the United States of America
by the Halliday Lithograph Corporation
West Hanover, Massachusetts

FOR
JAMES HAFLEY
AND
DANIEL BURKE
F.S.C.

I was of hir felaweshipe anon

The form is in *itself* as interesting, as active,
as much of the essence of the subject as the
idea, and yet so close is its fit and so inseparable its life that we catch it at no
moment on any errand of its own. That
verily is to *be* interesting—all round; that
is to be genuine and whole.

—Henry James
on Flaubert

1902

PREFACE

"Of all great writers," said Virginia Woolf of Jane Austen, "she is the most difficult to catch in the act of greatness." Nevertheless readers have not given up the pursuit. In the 1960s alone, some eight or nine books have already been published on Jane Austen, and older studies by Elizabeth Jenkins and Mary Lascelles, Marvin Mudrick and Andrew Wright have been reissued. The situation is much the same with individual essays: Lionel Trilling and Mark Schorer, Ian Watt and Reuben Brower, David Daiches and C. S. Lewis, and many less well-known critics have contributed introductions to this or that reprinting of an Austen novel or interpretations to one or another periodical or essay-collection. Inevitably, controversies have arisen. One critic disagrees with another; a second interpretation contradicts a first. In brief, one hundred and fifty years after her death, Jane Austen is causing a stir.

This book depends on just such a stir. It takes its life from controversy. Its starting point is problems.

I have chosen to deal with problems that are major in themselves: unity and parody in *Northanger Abbey*, irony and plot in *Pride and Prejudice*, morality and rigidity in *Mansfield Park*; and problems that lead inevitably to major issues: the place of Colonel Brandon in *Sense and Sensibility*, of Dick Musgrove and Mrs. Smith in *Persuasion*; the meaning of the ending of *Emma*. Since many of these problems have arisen because a critic holds a specific thesis about Jane Austen's novels, I have tried to bring them to a solution outside the conventional limits of a rigid thesis. It is undeniable that a thesis has the value of giving unity to a critical study and of calling attention to facets of an author's work that might otherwise be overlooked. But it can also be ruthless and operate like a steam roller, leveling what was meant to be anything but flat. Geoffrey Gorer's "central myth" ("the girl who hates and despises her mother and marries a father-surrogate") and H. W. Garrod's "one plot" ("a husband hunt . . . where the heroine marries the Muff") are singular examples of indiscriminate rolling along. But even Marvin Mudrick's more intellectually responsible thesis of irony as defense and discovery has had the unfortunate effect of making *Sense and Sensibility* and *Mansfield Park* look unrealistically thin.

I believe that if one approaches Jane Austen's novels on a less restricting basis the results will be more satisfactory. The premise of form provides such a basis because every meaning in a novel exists in a formal structure and every separate detail of the structure as well as the structure as a whole is necessarily meaningful. "The form is in *itself* as interesting, as active, as much of the essence of the subject as the idea, and yet so close is its fit and so inseparable its life that we catch it at no moment on any errand of its own," wrote Henry James. Therefore to concentrate on one aspect of a novel and to ask how it relates to others should be valuable. The premise, of course, cannot be that everything in a particular novel is perfectly fitting and that nothing is actually inconsistent. The premise is that everything *should* be related and *should* be relevant and that if something is not related and relevant, we *should* be able to say why it is not. What I deal with in the following chapters, then, are problems in Jane Austen's novels that have notably disturbed the critical intelligence of distinguished readers. I do this because I presume that what is seemingly or actually egregious can be read as a sign that reveals something important about a novel as a whole.

Though each of Jane Austen's novels introduces different problems, it soon becomes evident that the problems are in a sense all of a piece. They arise from the tension that exists between the demands of structural patterns and the demands of characters to be persons.

If one recognizes Fielding and Richardson as the chief formative influences on Jane Austen's fiction, one will also recognize why problems of pattern and person call into question the errand of form in her novels. Richardson was confused about many things, but he was convinced of the value of the individual person. Even in such a curiously muddled novel as *Pamela*, Richardson was able to distinguish the moral wrong of Mr. B— —'s attempting to seduce Pamela as less intolerable than his attempting to rape her. The threatened rape becomes so terrible an object in the novel that it is difficult not to interpret it symbolically. Pamela's physical violation becomes equated with her personal integrity. The novel is not so much about virtue rewarded as it is about integrity preserved. Pamela remains faithful to the inviolability of herself as a person. She insists that she must freely dispose of herself; she insists that Mr. B— — not use her wantonly.

There is a great deal that is painful in Richardson's morality, of course. Pamela seems ultimately to have sold herself, though the author and some of his readers remained innocent of the bargain. Sir Charles Grandison is so impossibly impeccable that one is sure that he is inhuman. And even the more wonderful and tragic Clarissa seems more than half in love with death. Physical integrity represents life to Clarissa, and rape death; therefore, she orders her coffin, places it in her room, lies down in it, and is eventually buried in it. Tragic though she may be, more than one critic has suspected her death to be connected with a death wish and her death wish to be connected with guilt feelings. But whatever one's interpretation may be, one thing is certain about Clarissa: she values the integrity of her person. She values it in such a way that violation of it by rape makes death inevitable. Pamela and Clarissa, and Harriet Byron after them, are individuals who will not remain quiet while bullies tamper with them and attempt to turn their radically individual persons into conveniently usable possessions. As acute a reader as Jane

Austen could hardly have eschewed the legacy of individuality and personality that Richardson left her.

The rambling Richardson gave way to the classically orientated Fielding and the epistolary gambol to the comic-epic march. Moral life was now to be viewed within a traditionally grounded framework: Fielding was implying by the use of his new structure that the comic epic itself was adequate to hold life within its limits and to judge the moral value of actions. In Fielding's novel Richardson's interior world gives way to external event and laughter replaces sentiment. The narrator sees life with the breadth of the epic poet and the more limited world of the letter writer disappears. Fielding attempts to make reality intelligible by drawing clear lines of cause and effect and by interpreting life through a literary structure and a conscious style rather than by presenting it, as Richardson attempted, in its seeming disorder. To Fielding it is possible to see life in terms of a structure that demands selectivity and still see it as real. Instead of giving everything that relates to one person, Fielding decides to give a few things that relate to everyone. His subject becomes the manners of mankind as seen in representative men, and he trusts in the comic epic, with its emphasis on the Ridiculous, to give meaningful artistic form to a picture of life.

Richardson's heroines and Fielding's form were a legacy of person and pattern for novelists who followed them, but they were a legacy of danger also. Richardson's attention to details of everyday life tended toward redundancy and formlessness. Fielding's attention to pattern and omniscient vision tended toward a neglect of that interiority which Richardson's thousands of pages weightily insisted could not be neglected. Where was the novelist who could do justice to both the personal and formal aspects of the novel? Sterne took a path all his own, and Smollett in his best novel toured England and Scotland and reflected both Fielding's and Richardson's influences without reducing the tension between pattern and person.

Jane Austen obviously did not see life in the manner of either Richardson or Fielding, but she did recognize the undeniable value of both novelists. She understood completely the importance of the individual and his interiority at the same time that she saw that the individual could live as an individual only in society and as a person only in relation to a moral order. Her novels, therefore, had to accommodate in their form the realistic demands of individuality, society, and morality.

Questions about individuality, society, and morality in Jane Austen's novels are inevitably questions of form in so far as form, in the words of Stallman and West, "represents the final unity of a work of fiction, the successful combining of all parts into an artful whole." My attempt in the following chapters is to show that there are pertinent problems that illuminate the errand of form in Jane Austen's novels because they ultimately call into question the relationship between patterns in the novels and the character of the persons who develop within those patterns. My attempt is to use these problems not only to show more precisely what Jane Austen was about when she was right but also to indicate and to estimate what she was about when she was wrong too.

I want to thank those who in different ways have helped me to complete this book. I am especially grateful to Professor James Hafley of St. John's University, New York, who many years ago introduced me to Jane Austen and who more recently read the manuscript of this book, suggested amendments, and bore— as only a good friend can—the moods and opinions of its author. To Daniel Burke, F.S.C., Academic Vice-President of La Salle College, Philadelphia, I am indebted in a way not easily measurable. Were it not for him, this book might never have been begun. I want also to thank Professor Ronald Christ of Manhattan College for his helpful criticism of an early version of the third chapter. To Andrew Noud, F.S.C., Director of the Cardinal

Hayes Library of Manhattan College, and his staff, especially
Mr. Robert Barry, Acquisitions Librarian, I am indebted for
many services. So am I likewise indebted to Edwin A. Quain, s.j.,
and George Fletcher of the Fordham University Press for their
help in preparing this manuscript for publication. I want more
generally to express my appreciation to my confrères at Manhattan College and my colleagues in the English Department for
their interest, their good humor, and their encouragement during
the last two years. Professor Eugene Law, f.s.c., deserves my
thanks for his careful reading of the galleys, as does Mrs. Mary
Ann O'Donnell for the preparation of the index.

I want, finally, to thank Oxford University Press for granting
me permission to quote from R. W. Chapman's third edition of
The Novels of Jane Austen and from his first edition of *The Works
of Jane Austen: Minor Works*.

CONTENTS

1   Unity and Parody in *Northanger Abbey*   1

2   The Mysteries of *Sense and Sensibility*   30

3   The Plot of *Pride and Prejudice*   60

4   Education and Integrity in *Mansfield Park*   86

5   Action and Symbol in *Emma*   109

6   Dignity and Duty in *Persuasion*   139

Notes   167

Index   187

THE ERRAND OF FORM

1

Unity and Parody in *Northanger Abbey*

Northanger Abbey has long been recognized as a burlesque of the Gothic novel, and rightly so; but that it finds its unity in such satire is more than questionable. Aside from the scattered references to Gothic novels in the Bath chapters, there is little evidence of an explicit parody being consistently shaped until Catherine Morland's visit with the Tilneys in Gloucestershire.[1] This is so evidently the case that one critic has proposed that *Northanger Abbey* is the result of combining two different stories to make a third.[2] And another has designated the problem of esthetic unity as the most crucial one in the novel.[3]

On the level of romantic action there is a more perceptible unity, for love comes first:

> [Catherine's] passion for ancient edifices was next in degree to her passion for Henry Tilney—and castles and abbies made usually the charm of those reveries which his image did not fill.[4]

Catherine Morland and Henry Tilney meet in Bath and are attracted to each other. At Northanger Abbey their love is fostered and then tried by General Tilney. At Fullerton the novel rounds out its emotional pattern when Henry proposes to Catherine. Within the perimeter of this action one finds the romantic life of Isabella Thorpe, which in its vain and devious way stands as a foil to the simple and straightforward love of Henry and Catherine. What is involved in this 'love story' from beginning to end, however, is certainly not peculiar to the typical Gothic tale.

Critics have generally recognized the problem of unity in

Northanger Abbey and have suggested different ways of solving it. Jane Austen's "problem," writes Marvin Mudrick, "is to write simultaneously a Gothic novel and a realistic novel, and to gain and keep the reader's acceptance of the latter while proving that the former is false and absurd."[5] These "two worlds must originate, converge, and be finally discriminated in the limited consciousness of that most ingenuous and domestic heroine, Catherine Morland."[6] The novel, of course, fails to sustain itself for this critic, who really is his own nemesis. He predetermines the solution of the problem of unity, does not find the solution he expects, and is consequently disappointed in *Northanger Abbey*.

Andrew Wright suggests that "Jane Austen shows us that though we must reject the Gothic world as inadequate and false, we cannot altogether apprehend the real world by good sense alone. Good sense [,] ironically, is limited too."[7] By indicating the inadequacy of good sense as Jane Austen's theme, Wright seems to be suggesting one way of viewing the whole of the novel. Howard Babb's approach is different:

> Whether Isabella or the Abbey supplies the local stimulus for Catherine, the source of her difficulties remains her own gullible imagination, which seizes on novels as statements of fact and therefore distorts the reality surrounding her. It is this strand of meaning that ties the halves of the story together, even though the parodic episode at the Abbey seems strained in comparison with the earlier, more realistic scenes at Bath.[8]

For Babb, Catherine Morland sees life imaginatively by way of a Gothic category and must be educated to see life as it really is and without any presuppositions. This argument is more convincing than Wright's. To conclude that Catherine and Henry need to learn about the obvious inadequacy of a life based on common sense alone seems too reductive a conclusion in light of the general intelligence of these lovers.[9] But Babb's solution is not completely adequate either. Walton Litz has argued against the repudiation of imagination in *Northanger Abbey*: Jane Austen's "criticism of Catherine's imagination is not that it is ridiculous or dangerous *per se*, but that it is uncontrolled by judgment."[10] And I cannot agree that Catherine Morland sees John and Isabella Thorpe by way of a Gothic category. As McKillop has observed, "She is docile and receptive, but unassuming good sense keeps her from a prompt and extreme adoption of romantic follies."[11] That same good sense keeps her "carefully dissociated from Isabella's use of sentimental and romantic clichés."[12] Catherine is at first just not sophisticated enough to see through the duplicity of the Thorpes' speech: "she had not been brought up . . . to know to how many idle assertions and impudent falsehoods the excess of vanity will lead"(65).

The problem of unity remains, then. The critics agree that *Northanger Abbey* parodies novels of the Gothic tradition and yet recognize that the parodic element in the novel is more sporadic than continuous. And the tenuous relation of the Gothic elements to the love story only complicates the problem. Clearly then any solution to the problem of unity in *Northanger Abbey* must assimilate both its romantic and its parodic elements into a pervasive pattern in the novel.[13]

The one major novelist before Jane Austen who faced a difficulty similar to hers and solved it in a masterly manner was Henry Fielding. He had to assimilate a parody of *Pamela* into a more important theme and a more elaborate structure when he wrote *Joseph Andrews*, and Jane Austen seems likely to have learned much from him. One may boggle at this and ask what her town-and-country life has to do with the roads and inns along Fielding's way. But Fielding's notion that the Ridiculous springs from affectation, which is itself rooted in vanity and hypocrisy,[14] seems certainly to have been used by Jane Austen in *Northanger Abbey*. Also, the corrupting influence of money on right conduct makes its presence painfully felt in both novels.

Moreover, there is in *Joseph Andrews* one episode that is so much like another in *Northanger Abbey* that we may legitimately conjecture that Jane Austen looked to Henry Fielding as a guide to make her way along the road of parody.

Fielding's "The History of Leonora, or the Unfortunate Jilt" is the story of a vain girl who engages herself to Horatio, a worthy young man, whom she jilts in his absence when Bellarmine happens along. There is even one sequence in this interpolated story of Leonora that is almost exactly duplicated in *Northanger Abbey*.

> In the evening an assembly was held, which Leonora honoured with her company; but intended to pay her dear Horatio the compliment of refusing to dance in his absence.
>
> O, why have not women as good resolution to maintain their vows as they have often good inclinations in making them!
>
> The gentleman who owned the coach and six came to the assembly. His clothes were as remarkably fine as his equipage could be. He soon attracted the eyes of the company; all the smarts, all the silk waistcoats with silver and gold edgings, were eclipsed in an instant.
>
> .   .   .   .
>
> The other ladies began to single out their former partners, all perceiving who would be Bellarmine's choice; which they however endeavoured, by all possible means, to prevent: many of them saying to Leonora, "O, madam! I suppose we shan't have the pleasure of seeing you dance tonight"; and then crying out, in Bellarmine's hearing, "O! Leonora will not dance, I assure you: her partner is not here." One maliciously attempted to prevent her, by sending a disagreeble fellow to ask her, that so she might be obliged either to dance with him, or sit down; but this scheme proved abortive. . . .
>
> . . . Bellarmine, having inquired who she was, advanced to her, and, with a low bow, begged the honour of dancing with her, which she, with as low a curtsy, immediately granted. She danced

with him all night, and enjoyed perhaps the highest pleasure that she was capable of feeling.[15]

In *Northanger Abbey* Isabella Thorpe finds herself in a similar situation with Captain Frederick Tilney when her fiancé, James Morland, is absent. Isabella, addressing Catherine on the subject of the ball, asks:

> "And must I go?"
> "Do not you intend it? I thought it was all settled."
> "Nay, since you make such a point of it, I can refuse you nothing. but do not insist upon my being very agreeable, for my heart, you know, will be some forty miles off. And as for dancing, do not mention it I beg; *that* is quite out of the question" (130).

At the dance that evening Henry Tilney is requested by his brother Frederick to ask Catherine whether her friend Isabella intends to dance at all. On the strength of her earlier conversation with Isabella, Catherine returns a negative answer:

> "Your brother will not mind it I know," said she, "because I heard him say before, that he hated dancing; but it was very good-natured in him to think of it. I suppose he saw Isabella sitting down, and fancied she might wish for a partner; but he is quite mistaken, for she would not dance upon any account in the world."
> Henry smiled, and said, "How very little trouble it can give you to understand the motive of other people's actions."
> "Why?—What do you mean?"
> "With you, it is not, How is such a one likely to be influenced? What is the inducement most likely to act upon such a person's feelings, age, situation, and probable habits of life considered?— but, how should *I* be influenced, what would be *my* inducement in acting so and so?"
> "I do not understand you."
> "Then we are on very unequal terms, for I understand you perfectly well."
> "Me?—yes; I cannot speak well enough to be unintelligible."
> "Bravo!—an excellent satire on modern language."

"But pray tell me what you mean."

"Shall I indeed?—Do you really desire it? —But you are not aware of the consequences; it will involve you in a very cruel embarrassment, and certainly bring on a disagreement between us."

"No, no; it shall not do either; I am not afraid."

"Well then, I only meant that your attributing my brother's wish of dancing with Miss Thorpe to good-nature alone, convinced me of your being superior in good-nature yourself to all the rest of the world."

Catherine blushed and disclaimed, and the gentleman's predictions were verified. There was a something, however, in his words which repaid her for the pain of confusion; and that something occupied her mind so much, that she drew back for some time, forgetting to speak or to listen, and almost forgetting where she was; till, roused by the voice of Isabella, she looked up and saw her with Captain Tilney preparing to give them hands across.

Isabella shrugged her shoulders and smiled, the only explanation of this extraordinary change which could at that time be given; but as it was not quite enough for Catherine's comprehension, she spoke her astonishment in very plain terms to her partner.

"I cannot think how it could happen! Isabella was so determined not to dance."

"And did Isabella never change her mind before?"

"Oh! But, because —— and your brother!—After what you told him from me, how could he think of going to ask her?"
(132–133)

As the plot of *Northanger Abbey* develops, the circumstantial character of events will change, but the method of exposing hypocrisy and vanity in them will remain the same. The method of making affectation look ridiculous by having actions speak louder than words Jane Austen found again and again to be the method of Fielding in *Joseph Andrews*.

Of course, this suggested relation of *Northanger Abbey* to *Joseph Andrews* does not solve the problem of unity in Jane Austen's novel. But the solution is certainly suggested by

Fielding's ingenious parody. The emphasis that Fielding places on words in *Joseph Andrews* is major. Leonora rejects out of hand the notion that the words she used to engage herself to Horatio meant anything at all. When Horatio happens in upon her and Bellarmine, Leonora remonstrates:

> "I know no pretensions a common acquaintance can have to lay aside the ceremonies of good breeding." "Sure," said he, "I am in a dream; for it is impossible I should be really esteemed a common acquaintance by Leonora, after what has passed between us!" "Passed between us! Do you intend to affront me before this gentleman?" "D--n me, affront the lady!" says Bellarmine, cocking his hat, and strutting up to Horatio: "does any man dare affront this lady before me, d--n me?" "Hark'ee, sir," says Horatio, "I would advise you to lay aside that fierce air; for I am mightily deceived if this lady has not a violent desire to get your worship a good drubbing." "Sir," said Bellarmine, "I have the honour to be her protector, and, d--n me, if I understand your meaning." "Sir," answered Horatio, "she is rather your protectress; but give yourself no more airs, for you see I am prepared for you" (shaking his whip at him). "O! *serviteur très humble*," says Bellarmine; "*Je vous entends parfaitement bien*." At which time the aunt, who had heard of Horatio's visit, entered the room, and soon satisfied all his doubts. She convinced him that he was never more awake in his life, and that nothing more extraordinary had happened in his three days' absence than a small alteration in the affections of Leonora; who now burst into tears, and wondered what reason she had given him to use her in so barbarous a manner.[16]

Leonora's promise to marry Horatio is as meaningful to her as her resolution not to dance in his absence. And if Leonora is here betrayed by her abuse of words, so too is Bellarmine. Fielding allows him to speak such an outrageous mishmash of French and English that we immediately recognize him as a high-class Mrs. Slipslop, who treats all to a specially scrambled hotchpotch of English and almost-English. Each in his own way is a "mighty affecter of hard words."[17] And both Leonora and Bellarmine show their vanity, hypocrisy, and avarice by their speech, which is a verbal correlate of their personal affectation. Fielding has created a Ridiculous style in *Joseph Andrews*—a style which shows the reality and the affectation simultaneously.

What we see in the story of the Unfortunate Jilt is true of the whole of *Joseph Andrews*. It is a book that takes life and measures life stylistically. An invocation of the deity is used to make Lady Booby's passion for Joseph look respectable until Fielding recalls it to reality:

> . . . The little god Cupid, fearing he had not yet done the lady's business, took a fresh arrow with the sharpest point out of his quiver, and shot it directly into her heart: in other and plainer language, the lady's passion got the better of her reason.[18]

An epic description turns a footman into a hero:

> Mr. Joseph Andrews was now in the one-and-twentieth year of his age. He was of the highest degree of middle stature. His limbs were put together with great elegance and no less strength. His legs and thighs were formed in the exactest proportion. His shoulders were broad and brawny; but yet his arms hung so easily, that he had all the symptoms of strength without the least clumsiness. His hair was of a nut-brown colour, and was displayed in wanton ringlets down his back. . . .[19]

Mrs. Slipslop, who always reaches for the big word, finds this Joseph "a strong healthy *luscious* boy enough"[20]; and her affectation gives Fielding just the right clue for a metamorphosis:

> As when a hungry tigress, who long has traversed the woods in fruitless search, sees within the reach of her claws a lamb, she prepares to leap on her prey; or as a voracious pike, of immense size, surveys through the liquid element a roach or gudgeon, which cannot escape her jaws, opens them wide to swallow the little fish; so did Mrs. Slipslop prepare to lay her violent amorous hands on the poor Joseph, when luckily her mistress's bell rung, and delivered the intended martyr from her clutches.[21]

Throughout *Joseph Andrews* a person's measure is taken by his words: the Great Promiser, for instance, is a liar; the man who speaks of courage to Abraham Adams is a coward; charity is redefined in terms of money: "Common charity, a f--t! . . . Common charity teaches us to provide for ourselves, and our families; and I and mine won't be ruined by your charity, I assure you," says the termagant Mrs. Tow-wouse to her generous husband.[22] In Fielding's novel the "respectable" Christian is shown by his speech to be, in Slipslop's words, "the Christian *specious*."[23] Jane Austen could hardly have missed the point that Fielding was making stylistically in *Joseph Andrews*; indeed, it seems that she did not.

The positive values in *Northanger Abbey*, like those in *Joseph Andrews*, are love and friendship; the negative, vanity and avarice. Also, as in Fielding's novel, these values are discriminated from each other as much by the way they are presented as by their being represented by different sets of characters. Henry and Eleanor Tilney (love and friendship) are straightforward, honest persons. They say what they mean. John and Isabella Thorpe and General Tilney (vanity and avarice) are deceitful and predatory. They say what they do not mean. Catherine Morland is at first not sophisticated enough to see through the duplicity of the Thorpes' speech, and her reaction to General Tilney is preconditioned by her reading of Mrs. Radcliffe. She does not see the general as he is; she sees him as she thinks he should be. He is to her one of those "visions of romance" (199) that she later shamefacedly puts by. He first deceives Catherine because she has already been deceived by Mrs. Radcliffe: "Charming as were all Mrs. Radcliffe's works . . . it was not in them perhaps that human nature . . . was to be looked for" (200). He later deceives her because she mistakes the man made of vanity and avarice for the gentleman he makes himself by his words.

The four who stand against love and friendship in Catherine Morland's life—John, Isabella, General Tilney, and Mrs. Radcliffe—offend in their speech and give the lie to reality. This is so completely the case that I want to suggest that Jane Austen gives unity to *Northanger Abbey* by a thematic preoccupation with the question of speech as it relates to different characters in the novel. The plot of *Northanger Abbey* turns on Catherine's gradual discrimination of word from reality in the speeches of John and Isabella Thorpe, General Tilney and Mrs. Radcliffe. Whereas all of Jane Austen's novels are concerned with words, *Northanger Abbey* is preeminent in dramatizing that concern. Indeed, one may borrow a sentence from Henry James and say that in *Northanger Abbey* "all life comes back to the question of our speech, the medium through which we communicate with one another."[24]

Henry Tilney is a normative character and he displays an interest in the precise use of language throughout *Northanger Abbey*. Catherine Morland's introduction to Henry is made delightful by his taking his hobby-horse over the language hurdles of a conventional first meeting. After chatting with Catherine for some time, Henry apologizes for not putting her through the normal initiation prescribed for young ladies:

> "You need not give yourself that trouble, sir."
> "No trouble I assure you, madam." Then forming his features into a set smile, and affectedly softening his voice, he added, with a simpering air, "Have you been long in Bath, madam?"
> "About a week, sir," replied Catherine, trying not to laugh.
> "Really!" with affected astonishment.
> "Why should you be surprized, sir?"
> "Why, indeed!" said he, in his natural tone—"but some emotion must appear to be raised by your reply, and surprize is more easily assumed, and not less reasonable than any other.— Now let us go on. Were you never here before, madam?"
> "Never, sir."
> "Indeed! Have you yet honoured the Upper Rooms?"
> "Yes, sir, I was there last Monday."

"Have you been to the theatre?"

"Yes, sir, I was at the play on Tuesday."

"To the concert?"

"Yes, sir, on Wednesday."

"And are you altogether pleased with Bath?"

"Yes—I like it very well."

"Now I must give one smirk, and then we may be rational again" (25–26).

To Henry this is a ritual of word-nonsense that is irrational because it is personally meaningless.

Henry switches from a ridicule of conventional conversational habits to "the usual style of letter-writing among women," which he finds "faultless, except in three particulars." "And what are they?" "A general deficiency of subject, a total in-attention to stops, and a very frequent ignorance of grammar" (27). And before their first meeting ends, Henry recalls to Catherine the proper relation of word to reality.

> Catherine feared . . . that he indulged himself a little too much with the foibles of others.—"What are you thinking of so earnestly?" said he, as they walked back to the ball-room. . . .
>
> Catherine coloured, and said, "I was not thinking of any thing."
>
> "That is artful and deep, to be sure; but I had rather be told at once that you will not tell me."
>
> "Well then, I will not" (29).

This then is Catherine's first meeting with Henry Tilney. The first time he is presented Henry scores conventional conversation as "irrational"; champions syntax and grammar; and insists on directness in speech, as opposed to what is "artful and deep." It is also clear, as Henry canters before Catherine, that she is amused by him and that they like each other very much. So from the beginning Henry's devotion to a reasonable use of language improves his relationship to Catherine.

Henry Tilney does not stable his hobby-horse after Chapter III.

Rather he rides it through the whole of *Northanger Abbey*. He continues to debunk the same species of chatter that he attacked in his first dialogue with Catherine. He prizes Catherine's "fresh feelings" and unaffected speech: "Oh! who can ever be tired of Bath?" (79). He deplores the dishonesty of those whose affectation leads them to debunk what they like:

> "Bath, compared with London, has little variety, and so every body finds out every year. 'For six weeks, I allow Bath is pleasant enough; but beyond *that*, it is the most tiresome place in the world.' You would be told so by people of all descriptions, who come regularly every winter, lengthen their six weeks into ten or twelve, and go away at last because they can afford to stay no longer" (78).

Henry, like the narrator in Chapter 5, deplores "the common cant" (38). The narrator finds that in novels "the liveliest effusions of wit and humor are conveyed to the world in the best chosen language" (38). Henry declares that the "person, be it gentleman or lady, who has not pleasure in a good novel, must be intolerably stupid" (106). He thoroughly understands the speech of Isabella and John Thorpe and of his father. And he suggests to Catherine why she is easily taken in by their words: ". . . your mind is warped by an innate principle of general integrity . . ." (219). Catherine puts it another way: "I cannot speak well enough to be unintelligible." Henry's reply is knowledgeable: "Bravo!—an excellent satire on modern language" (133). Henry clearly sees that language is used by many people to clothe their vanity and avarice in acceptable clichés. He also sees that the less-than-worldly-wise Catherine is too inexperienced to see as clearly as he does.

Henry continues, after their first interview, to show Catherine the propriety of precision in speech. He first, as was seen, objected to her saying "I was not thinking of any thing." Other expressions are given the same careful scrutiny. Catherine says to Henry, "I really thought . . . young men despised novels

amazingly." Henry immediately takes possession of the word:
"It is *amazingly*; it may well suggest *amazement* if they do—
for they read nearly as many as women" (107). The word to
Catherine is simply a convenient trite expression. It is Isabella
Thorpe's favorite word and she has insinuated it into Catherine's
vocabulary by her persistent and affected use of it. As soon as
Henry takes the word from Catherine, he pumps some meaning
into it by defining it in relation to the substantive, "amazement."
He does the same with "nice." Catherine remarks, "But now
really, do not you think Udolpho the nicest book in the world?"

> "The nicest;—by which I suppose you mean the neatest. That
> must depend upon the binding."
> "Henry," said Miss Tilney, "you are very impertinent. Miss
> Morland, he is treating you exactly as he does his sister. He is for
> ever finding fault with me, for some incorrectness of language, and
> now he is taking the same liberty with you. The word 'nicest,' as
> you used it, did not suit him; and you had better change it as soon
> as you can, or we shall be overpowered with Johnson and Blair all
> the rest of the way" (107–108).

Henry is not easily dismayed by his sister's finally calling him
"more nice than wise" (108), and in a very few minutes he is
drawing careful distinctions between "to torment" and "to
instruct" (109–110). Later, in the same chapter, Henry finds
that he must mediate between Catherine's use of "horrid" and
his sister's understanding of the word (112–113). At Northanger,
Henry again takes Catherine to task when she is disappointed
by Isabella's failing to send the letter that she had "promised
so faithfully to write" (195). "Promised so faithfully—A
faithful promise!—That puzzles me.—I have heard of a faithful
performance. But a faithful promise—the fidelity of promising!
It is a power little worth knowing however, since it can deceive
and pain you" (196).

Jane Austen is certainly not trying to make her hero sound

crochety at the age of five-and-twenty. Nor is she simply creating humor out of verbal situations. Generally speaking, Catherine's misuse of words like "nicest" and "torment" is without guile. Because of her own integrity she is not quick to suspect the guile of others like Isabella, who purposely misuse words to deceive. Furthermore, the misuse of words can function dramatically in other ways. "Amazingly," for instance, shows that Catherine has come under the influence of Isabella and that she has not discerned the reality behind the verbal construct. She has discerned neither the substantive "amazement" behind "amazingly" nor the substance of Isabella behind the façade of the verbally constructed Miss Thorpe. The mix-up between Catherine and Eleanor over "horrid" occurs because Catherine speaks of the verbal reality of a Gothic horror novel in such vivid terms that Eleanor interprets "horrid" as referring to a real-life situation, not a fictional one. Eleanor's mistake is a foreshadowing of Catherine's at Northanger Abbey when she imposes a fictional construct on a life situation. "Faithful promise" defines Isabella perfectly because it suggests her limitations. She is a faithful promiser but an unfaithful performer. Jane Austen carefully turns Henry's passion for precision into a dramatic device to pinpoint the motives of characters and to suggest the general drama of word and deed that runs through *Northanger Abbey*.

While Henry is aware of the ways that language can be misused, he is also aware of how it can be pleasantly played with. After his championing of correctness at the expense of Catherine and Eleanor, his sister requires him to tell Catherine "that you think very highly of the understanding of women" (113). Henry replies, "Miss Morland, no one can think more highly of the understanding of women than I do. In my opinion, nature has given them so much, that they never find it necessary to use more than half" (114). Henry can also play more elaborate word-games. He is able to sustain a comparison of dancing to marriage over two pages of dialogue (76–78), and he spins a tale of Gothic horrors at Northanger Abbey that is good enough to give Catherine a momentary fright (Chapter 20).[25] All this word-play is functional of course. The intelligence of Catherine is at times only partially in evidence in the novel. She especially seems to want for wit when she confronts Northanger and General Tilney with *Udolpho* as her Baedecker. In Gloucester-shire Henry's Gothic account of the abbey gives zest to Catherine's investigations. And Henry's comparison of marriage with dancing is found to be very apt when applied to Isabella's fidelity to James Morland, both in her promise to marry him and her promise not to dance in his absence.

When Henry is looked at with respect to his concern for language, he is seen to be totally aware of reality because he is perceptive and also because he is thoroughly aware of the use and abuse of the speech medium through which reality is inter-preted. Catherine is fortunate to meet Henry so early on in her stay at Bath because she needs the kind of guidance he gives her. She is a very unworldly creature and consequently she is sus-ceptible to subterfuge. She is "open, candid, artless, guileless, with affections strong but simple, forming no pretensions, and knowing no disguise" (206). Although she might misuse words like "amazingly" or "nicest" and be taken in by words like "dearest" and "sweetest," she is absolutely faithful to her word once she gives it. When Catherine realizes that John Thorpe has tricked her into riding with him to Blaize Castle by lying about the Tilneys' driving to Wick Rocks (86), she is aroused to indignation because she had pledged herself to walk with them:

> "How could you say, that you saw them driving up the Lansdown-road?—I would not have had it happen so for the world.—They must think it so strange; so rude of me! to go by them, too, without saying a word! You do not know how vexed I am.—I shall have no pleasure at Clifton, nor in any thing else. I had rather, ten thou-sand times rather get out now, and walk back to them. How could you say, you saw them driving out in a phaeton?" (87)

She is so unashamedly honest that she later tells Henry that "if Mr. Thorpe would only have stopped, I would have jumped out and run after you" (94). On another day, after having promised to walk with Henry and Eleanor, she stoutly refuses to break her appointment to satisfy the Thorpes and her brother James. When John Thorpe takes it upon himself to excuse her to the Tilneys, Catherine becomes suitably indignant: " 'If I could not be persuaded into doing what I thought wrong, I never will be tricked into it.' And with these words she broke away and hurried off" (101). Catherine's word is her bond; she means what she says. And because of "an innate principle of general integrity," she expects others to mean what they say too. Catherine however is doomed to disappointment.

Northanger Abbey makes clear that people do not generally lack vanity and avarice. Consequently they have little respect for the truth. That is why exceptions like Eleanor and Catherine are singled out for special mention:

> Miss Tilney met her with great civility, returned her advances with equal good will, and they continued talking together as long as both parties remained in the room; and though in all probability not an observation was made, nor an expression used by either which had not been made and used some thousands of times before, under that roof, in every Bath season, yet the merit of their being spoken with simplicity and truth, and without personal conceit, might be something uncommon (72).

Isabella is the opposite of these two girls. She is Jane Austen's reincarnation of Fielding's Leonora. She plays two men against each other to get the better fortune, flattering herself all the while that she is worth every extra guinea she can marry into. John Thorpe is conceited enough to think that Catherine without doubt will marry him as soon as he proposes. He wants her as his bride because he thinks her rich in her own right and heiress to the Allen fortune as well. And General Tilney wants Catherine for a daughter-in-law for the very same reasons. When he turns her out of Northanger, we find that "she was guilty only of being less rich than he had supposed her to be" (244). Catherine in the midst of it all bespeaks her integrity when she says, ". . . to marry for money I think the wickedest thing in existence" (124). For those given to duplicity Catherine is a natural victim:

> Her own family were plain matter-of-fact people, who seldom aimed at wit of any kind; her father, at the utmost, being contented with a pun, and her mother with a proverb; they were not in the habit therefore of telling lies to increase their importance, or of asserting at one moment what they would contradict the next (65–66).

Much of the humor of the novel comes, therefore, in consequence of Catherine's encounters with the Thorpes because they are what she is not.

Isabella and John have no regard for the meaning of words or for propriety in using them. Isabella is a great offender with adjectives and adverbs and has an affection for superlatives. "Dearest, sweetest Catherine" is Isabella's "best and oldest" friend (98). After her engagement to James, Isabella pronounces herself "the happiest of mortals" (121). She uses the words "so" and "amazingly" as the careless cook does handfuls of salt: "I scold them all amazingly" (40), "something amazingly insipid about her" (41), "so amazingly impatient to begin" (52), "so immoderately sick of Bath" (70), "amazingly shocking to be sure" (90), "a friend who loved her so dearly" (98), "I , who love you so excessively" (98), "never saw any body so handsome before" (118), "amazingly conceited" (135), "amazingly glad" (143), "amazingly absent" (144), "so amazingly changeable and inconstant" (146), "so amazingly tired" (147), and so on and so forth. Isabella is also poor at addition. She tells Catherine that she has drawn up a list of ten or twelve Gothic novels for her. "What are they all?" asks Catherine. The "all" of "ten or twelve" proves to be seven (40). A "few minutes" become "at least three hours" for Isabella. She often has a "thousand things to say" (62). A few minutes' wait turns into "ages" rather quickly (67). "Two years and a half" are "endless" (136). Add a dash of things that are "odious" and a smattering of those that are "monstrous"; put in some that happen "always" or "never"; finish with the "most" or "least" of something else and you have the ingredients of Isabella's potpourri of affectation. Her speech is an undeviating tribute to imprecision: it is especially apt at expressing feelings that do not exist. One has only to reread Isabella's letter to Catherine (216–218) to find her misuse of language in a nutshell. Catherine finally sums her up accurately when she says simply, "She is a vain coquette" (218).

John Thorpe has mastered "damn" in the same way that his sister has "amazingly". (His continual use of "damn" suggests his relation to Bellarmine and is another instance of Jane Austen's possible debt to Fielding.) He is even bold enough to reach for a cognate: "a d----- thing to be miserly" (89). He sprinkles his bravado with incivility:

> "Ah, mother! how do you do?" said he, giving her a hearty shake of the hand: "where did you get that quiz of a hat, it makes you look like an old witch?" (49).
> On his two younger sisters he then bestowed an equal portion of his fraternal tenderness, for he asked each of them how they did, and observed that they both looked very ugly (49).
> "Old Allen is as rich as a Jew—is not he?" Catherine did not understand him—and he repeated his question, adding in explanation, "Old Allen, the man you are with."
> "Oh! Mr. Allen, you mean. Yes, I believe, he is very rich" (63).

John's speech accurately indicates that he is much impressed with himself and little impressed with anyone else. He is quick to damn and to insult, and slow to perceive and to understand.

He and his sister are foreigners in the land of Johnson and Blair: a "nice" use of language is beyond "amazingly" and "damn."

The disregard for the meanings of words in the speech of John and Isabella is also witnessed to by their deeds in relation to their words. This was already seen when Isabella danced with Frederick Tilney after she said that she would not dance in the absence of James Morland. Moreover, Isabella's simultaneous pursuit of both Morland and Captain Tilney is given in capsule form when she pursues two other men. When she professes to be running away from them, she is actually running after them:

> "Well, I am amazingly glad I have got rid of them! And now, what say you to going to Edgar's Buildings with me, and looking at my new hat? You said you should like to see it."
>
> Catherine readily agreed. "Only," she added, "perhaps we may overtake the two young men."
>
> "Oh! never mind that. If we make haste, we shall pass by them presently, and I am dying to shew you my hat."
>
> "But if we only wait a few minutes, there will be no danger of seeing them at all."
>
> "I shall not pay them any such compliment, I assure you. I have no notion of treating men with such respect. *That* is the way to spoil them" (43).

Isabella's most flagrant disregard of word in relation to deed follows her engagement to James Morland. Having promised to marry him and having insisted that "the smallest income in nature would be enough for me" (119), she breaks the engagement because Morland's fortune is smaller than she estimated. Isabella expresses her new attitude toward money when she says, ". . . it is not a trifle that will support a family now-a-days; and after all that romancers may say, there is no doing without money" (146). As to her promise of marriage, this premonition seems fair warning: "What one means one day, you know, one may not mean the next. Circumstances change, opinions alter" (146). James's letter announcing the broken engagement indicates

that circumstances have changed. Isabella's letter to Catherine
some days later shows that circumstances have altered once again.
Captain Tilney, weary of his skirmish, has beaten a retreat. But
Catherine is not now to be imposed on. Isabella is permitted to
follow in the footsteps of Leonora. The romantic Slipslop
pronounces a fitting epitaph for both young ladies: "Why I
must own . . . the gentleman was a little false-hearted; but
howsumever, it was hard to have two lovers, and get never a
husband at all."[26]

John disregards the relation of word to deed as flagrantly as his
sister does. The only thing that signifies for Thorpe is that he is
either pleased or magnified by his use of words:

> He took out his watch: "How long do you think we have been
> running it from Tetbury, Miss Morland?"
>
> "I do not know the distance." Her brother told her that it was
> twenty-three miles.
>
> "*Three*-and-twenty!" cried Thorpe; "five-and-twenty if it is an
> inch." Morland remonstrated, pleaded the authority of road-books,
> innkeepers, and milestones; but his friend disregarded them all; he
> had a surer test of distance. "I know it must be five-and-twenty,"
> said he, "by the time we have been doing it. It is now half after
> one; we drove out of the inn-yard at Tetbury as the town-clock
> struck eleven; and I defy any man in England to make my horse go
> less than ten miles an hour in harness; that makes it exactly
> twenty-five."
>
> "You have lost an hour," said Morland; "it was only ten
> o'clock when we came from Tetbury" (45).

The quick trip from Tetbury suggests the quality of John's
horses and the excellence of their owner and driver. But as soon
as these things are established, John initiates his conquest of
Catherine by inviting her to ride with him the next day:

> "I will drive you up Lansdown Hill to-morrow."
>
> "Thank you; but will not your horse want rest?"
>
> "Rest! he has only come three-and-twenty miles to-day . . ." (47).

Mileage shrinks and horses slow down because John Thorpe wants the pleasure of Catherine's company. There is no norm for his words outside of himself. They are, as the narrator describes them, "the effusions of his endless conceit" (66).

"Have you ever read Udolpho, Mr. Thorpe?" Catherine asks quite innocently.

> "Udolpho! Oh, Lord! not I; I never read novels; I have something else to do."
>
> Catherine, humbled and ashamed, was going to apologize for her question, but he prevented her by saying, "Novels are all so full of nonsense and stuff; there has not been a tolerably decent one come out since Tom Jones, except the Monk; I read that t'other day; but as for all the others, they are the stupidest things in creation."
>
> "I think you must like Udolpho, if you were to read it; it is so very interesting."
>
> "Not I, faith! No, if I read any, it shall be Mrs. Radcliff's; her novels are amusing enough; they are worth reading; some fun and nature in *them*."
>
> "Udolpho was written by Mrs. Radcliff," said Catherine, with some hesitation, from the fear of mortifying him (48–49).

This kind of aberration is more than humorous; it is at times dangerous. John lies to Catherine about the Tilneys' abandoning her so that he might take her to Clifton. (Too long a trip, incidentally, for his slow horses!) John lies to the Tilneys about Catherine's having a previous engagement so that he can set out with her a second time for Blaize Castle. John's most notorious lie is told to General Tilney. He describes Catherine as an heiress because he thinks he deserves one and because he feels that it will add to his prestige with the general:

> his vanity induced him to represent the family as yet more wealthy than his vanity and avarice had made him believe them. With whomsoever he was, or was likely to be connected, his own consequence

always required that theirs should be great, and as his intimacy with any acquaintance grew, so regularly grew their fortune (244–245).

But Catherine's refusal to marry him leads Thorpe to turn her into a pauper. His prestidigitation leads General Tilney to turn Catherine out of his house.

Northanger Abbey develops then by repeating a serial kind of structure: (1) something is said (Isabella says she is running away from two men: Isabella says money is of no importance in her life; Isabella says she will marry James; John says Tetbury is twenty-five miles away; John says he does not read novels; John says the Tilneys have abandoned Catherine; John says Catherine has a previous engagement; John says Catherine is rich and then later says that she is poor); (2) reality intervenes to give the lie to what was said; (3) the deed is related to the word and a judgment is then made. At length, the explicit judgments on the situation become Catherine's. She is educated to reality: "We must live and learn," remarks Mrs. Morland (236), and that is just what Catherine does in *Northanger Abbey*.

This serial structure operates in relation to a more total systematic structure. Catherine comes to Bath and meets those whom she must learn to judge: Isabella Thorpe, John Thorpe, Mrs. Radcliffe, and General Tilney. As the role of John and Isabella becomes less important that of General Tilney becomes more important. He is motivated by vanity and avarice in the same way that they are. He seeks to satisfy these vices by having his children make financially spectacular marriages that will reflect notably on his name and reputation. Isabella and John want to marry for the same kind of satisfaction. Isabella's sycophantic relation to Catherine is nicely duplicated by the general's flattery of her. And John Thorpe's insulting way is repeated in the general's turning Catherine out of doors. Indeed, Jane Austen tars and feathers both General Tilney and John

Thorpe with down from the same pillow: the true account of
Catherine's family and fortune taught the general

> that he had been scarcely more misled by Thorpe's first boast of the
> family wealth, than by his subsequent malicious overthrow of it;
> that in no sense of the word were they necessitous or poor, and
> that Catherine would have three thousand pounds. This was so
> material an amendment of his late expectations, that it greatly
> contributed to smooth the descent of his pride; and by no means
> without its effect was the private intelligence, which he was at
> some pains to procure, that the Fullerton estate, being entirely at
> the disposal of its present proprietor, was consequently open to
> every greedy speculation (251–252).

General Tilney is clearly caught here by Jane Austen in the
pattern of saying-doing-judging that she uses to characterize the
Thorpes. The general treats Catherine with great deference:

> The general attended her himself to the street-door, saying every
> thing gallant as they went down stairs, admiring the elasticity of her
> walk, which corresponded exactly with the spirit of her dancing,
> and making her one of the most graceful bows she had ever beheld,
> when they parted (103).

And this deference is lasting—for a while. General Tilney is
solicitous that Catherine eat well (154), that she remain "safe
and dry" (177), that the path on which she walks be not too
damp (179), that "any necessity should rob him even for an
hour of Miss Morland's company" (220). The trip to London,
which so robs him, puts him in John Thorpe's presence. The
general returns and turns Catherine out of Northanger with the
utmost lack of civility. But this is to be expected. He constantly
gives the lie to his words. The outing to Woodston is a clue to
his later and more portentous contradiction of word by deed.

   When the general elects to visit Henry at Woodston with
Catherine and Eleanor as his companions, he tells Henry, "Well,
well, we will take our chance some one of those days. There

is no need to fix." Then he fixes: "But on Wednesday, I think, Henry, you may expect us . . . about a quarter before one . . ." (210). As to food, the general is willing to take potluck. Henry interprets to the girls, "I must go and prepare a dinner for you to be sure" (211). He leaves on Sunday to be ready by Wednesday. Catherine is bewildered because she takes the general at his word:

> That he was very particular in his eating, she had, by her own unassisted observation, already discovered; but why he should say one thing so positively, and mean another all the while, was most unaccountable! How were people, at that rate, to be understood? Who but Henry could have been aware of what his father was at?

Wednesday puts Henry's interpretation to the test:

> She could not but observe that the abundance of the dinner did not seem to create the smallest astonishment in the General; nay, that he was even looking at the side-table for cold meat which was not there. His son and daughter's observations were of a different kind. They had seldom seen him eat so heartily at any table but his own; and never before known him so little disconcerted by the melted butter's being oiled (214–215).

General Tilney has all the integrity of a John or Isabella Thorpe, and his son knows it and knows exactly how to deal with him.

Henry is not only his father's interpreter but his antithesis as well. The general may go back on his word, but Henry will not:

> He felt himself bound as much in honour as in affection to Miss Morland, and believing that heart to be his own which he had been directed [by his father] to gain, no unworthy retraction of a tacit consent, no reversing decree of unjustifiable anger, could shake his fidelity, or influence the resolutions it prompted (247).

Henry, who has disclaimed cant and championed precision, refuses to be false to his word. Catherine was once willing to run after him when John Thorpe gave the lie to her honor; now

Henry runs after Catherine—all the way to Fullerton—when his father gives the lie to his honor. Love and friendship will not be meaningless to Catherine as long as Henry Tilney can interpret them to her.

Catherine's adventure at Northanger is an encounter with reality. It becomes a purgative of romance. It shows that Mrs. Radcliffe's world is papier-mâché, just as are the personae of Isabella, John, and General Tilney. After reading *The Mysteries of Udolpho* at Bath, Catherine comes to Northanger Abbey expecting to find in reality what she read about in a horror novel. Here the Gothic world of Mrs. Radcliffe is exposed to the pattern of word-reality-judgment that the Thorpes and General Tilney were exposed by. The word pattern is not strict Radcliffe: there is no door in the bed chamber that leads to a secret stairway and that cannot be locked from inside; there is no real black veil to be lifted. But there is a chest and a cabinet and a mysterious room. The chest and the cabinet are anticipated by Henry Tilney's tale, which is mock-Radcliffe: "Oh! Mr. Tilney, how frightful!— This is just like a book," cries Catherine (159). And each incident is just another way of lifting the dreaded black veil: the chest reveals a counterpane, the closet reveals laundry bills, and the mysterious room in which Mrs. Tilney died reveals reality. After Henry's mild reproach—"Remember the country and the age in which we live. Remember that we are English, that we are Christians"—Catherine "with tears of shame . . . ran off to her own room" (197–198).

The next chapter begins, "The visions of romance were over. Catherine was completely awakened" (99). She realizes that the "sort of reading which she had . . . indulged" in had misled her. She judges that

> charming as were all of Mrs. Radcliffe's works, and charming even as were the works of all her imitators, it was not in them perhaps that human nature, at least in the midland counties of England, was to be looked for (200).

Catherine, her country, and her acquaintances prove that Mrs. Radcliffe's novels are verbal constructs that have no relation to any known reality. And precisely as that kind of verbal construct do they relate to the Thorpes and General Tilney. Isabella as the friend of "dearest, sweetest Catherine" and as the "happiest of mortals" as James Morland's fiancée is word-made not real. John Thorpe as a skilled horseman, an Oxford trencherman, and as a man "quite in love" with Catherine—not her fortune—is word-made, not real. General Tilney as a courteous and solicitous friend of Catherine's is word-made, not real. Once Catherine sees the Radcliffe world as a world of words, she sees characters in the real world as word-made too: letters from James and Isabella reveal the real Isabella; an eleven-hour trip from Gloucestershire to Fullerton reveals the real General Tilney; an explanation from Henry reveals the real John Thorpe. Once Catherine learns how to read the Radcliffe kind of fiction in relation to reality, she soon learns how to read the Thorpe and General Tilney kind of fiction as well. The Gothic parody in *Northanger Abbey* correlates perfectly with the realism of false friendship and love. In both cases the attempt to substitute a word-construct for real life is exposed.

Robert Liddell objected to the Gothic parody because Catherine "was banished from Northanger on account of the General's illusions, not her own."[27] But perhaps that is not the point at all. Catherine's encounter with her Radcliffe fancies at Northanger develops her character and Henry's as well. When Henry spins the Gothic tale, he is seen to be a man who understands how words work creatively. His story supplements his passion for Johnson and Blair. He proves himself imaginative as well as perceptive and precise. His benevolence toward Catherine after her suspicions of his father shows a gentleness and sympathy hitherto unexplored in the novel. Catherine, on her side, is intellectually and emotionally enriched by the exposure of her follies. Therefore, when one fits the Gothic parody into the plot and character development of the Henry–Catherine love story, the whole novel makes sense. If one presumes that the love story must fit into a larger pattern of parody, the novel will make little sense at all.

From the beginning of *Northanger Abbey*, Catherine is called the heroine. She is the heroine precisely because she is atypical of the Gothic heroine. Jane Austen suggests that the problems which a true heroine must face stem from the passions of men, not from closets, chests, and mysterious rooms. Jane Austen throws away the Gothic mold for heroines and supplies a new realistic one of her own. The Gothic pattern is seen to be a distortion of personality; the realistic pattern is the making of a person. Catherine's encounters with closets, chests, and mysterious rooms stem from a curiosity engendered by reading. Jane Austen uses Gothic novels in *Northanger Abbey* in the same way that another novelist might use another kind of misdirection as the cause of mistaken conduct in another novel. Mrs. Radcliffe and her imitators warp Catherine's mind until Henry sets it straight again. Her heroism is really tested after this straightening point when she is forced to deal with the hardships that follow from the vanity and avarice of the Thorpes and the general. This is so completely the case that Henry is able to marry Catherine because his father is consistently vicious:

> The circumstance which chiefly availed, was the marriage of his daughter with a man of fortune and consequence, which took place in the course of the summer—an accession of dignity that threw him into a fit of good-humour, from which he did not recover till after Eleanor had obtained his forgiveness of Henry, and his permission for him "to be a fool if he liked it!" (250)

The true hero and heroine patiently defy the passions of a man, not the dangers of a haunted house. Also, characteristically, the truth about Catherine's family and fortune leads the general to begin rebuilding his verbal persona:

On the strength of this [information], the General, soon after Eleanor's marriage, permitted his son to return to Northanger, and thence made him the bearer of his consent, very courteously worded in a page full of empty professions to Mr. Morland (252).

To the very last paragraph of *Northanger Abbey* Jane Austen sustains the drama of word versus deed. General Tilney, in the name of what and whom he stands for, is permitted to commit his last characteristic outrage on the language.

To the very end the abuse of language distinguishes the insincerity of General Tilney, as it had that of the Thorpes before him. The flattering word and the hyperbolic phrase clothe the otherwise naked cupidity and conceit of the general, Isabella, and John. For all its high spirits, *Northanger Abbey* from start to finish is concerned with the values of love and friendship, sincerely and accurately shown and expressed by Henry and Eleanor and Catherine; with the vices of vanity and avarice, expressed in the hypocrisy and lies of the general and John and Isabella. Words then are important throughout *Northanger Abbey* because their choice and their relation to reality distinguish true from false and good from bad.

Northanger Abbey, of course, is not the only novel of Jane Austen's that dramatizes a concern for words. "Eleanor and Marianne" became *Sense and Sensibility*, a novel in which the relation of "love" and "esteem" is dramatized. "First Impressions" became *Pride and Prejudice*,[28] a novel which insists on the importance of "justice" and "gratitude." In addition, *Emma* can be read as an extended definition of "true gentility" and *Mansfield Park* of "education." *Persuasion* explores the meaning of "dignity" and "duty." Jane Austen was tirelessly concerned with taking words out of the dictionary and putting them into reality. Their meaning in her novels is defined by experiences that draw on reason, sympathy, and affection and that temper character and personality. But in no novel is her concern for words as morally and esthetically pervasive as it is in *Northanger Abbey*, where mastery of language becomes the outward aspect of Catherine Morland's radical human effort to mature. Therefore, in no subsequent novel of Jane Austen's will one find a heroine so lost for words that her moral and emotional integrity will be seen, as Catherine's is, in a face in which "the eight parts of speech shone out most expressively" from "her eyes" (120).

2

The Mysteries of *Sense and Sensibility*

Critics unanimously regret at least one episode in *Sense and Sensibility*—Colonel Brandon's revelation of Willoughby's past to Elinor Dashwood. This unfortunate episode, B. C. Southam suggests, is a residue of the epistolary form of "Elinor and Marianne." He finds a "weakness of . . . structure and writing . . . noticeable when Jane Austen uses the conventional patterns of sentimental and romantic melodrama" in "the Colonel Brandon-Eliza-Willoughby sub-plot. . . ."[1] For Ian Watt "there is certainly an unconvincing quality about Brandon, especially when he tells all to Elinor. . . ."[2] Walton Litz calls the recital a "hackneyed tale,"[3] and to Howard Babb it is "stylistically gross."[4] "There is a single occasion," observes Marvin Mudrick, "on which Colonel Brandon speaks at some length: when he tells all regarding Willoughby. . . . The sad fact is . . . that just at this point Jane Austen's control of her subject collapses utterly."[5]

On other matters a consensus is less available. To Ian Watt the form of *Sense and Sensibility* derives from "domestic comedy, . . . a characteristically English literary genre," and he finds in the novel a "lightness of manner [that] may lead us to underestimate its real scope."[6] For Watt the scope is nothing less than the problem of the dissociation of sensibility, and its roots the antithetical philosophies of Locke and Shaftesbury. To Walton Litz the novel derives from "the rigid antithetical form" of "late eighteenth-century moralistic fiction."[7] He finds that a "depressing atmosphere . . . hangs over . . . much of *Sense and Sensibility* . . . ."[8] Litz hints at a conceptual grounding, through Maria Edgeworth, in Adam Smith's *Theory of Moral Sentiments*, "where the

Stoical system of self-command is opposed to the Benevolent system of sympathetic indulgence."[9]

Perhaps the most interesting disagreement between these two critics is one that brings to mind the most important of critical problems—the problem of what *Sense and Sensibility* is about. An original review of the novel, which appeared in *The British Critic*, suggested that "the object of the work is to represent the effects on the conduct of life, of discreet quiet good sense on the one hand, and an over-refined and excessive susceptibility on the other."[10] Now some critics maintain that sense and sensibility are meant to remain apart in the novel; others that they are meant to join hands. In Marvin Mudrick's view, "Not merely *false* feeling, but feeling itself, is bad" in the novel.[11] "Edward Ferrars and Colonel Brandon represent, in fact, the antidote to feeling, the proposition that the only cure for a passionate heart is to remove it."[12] A slightly, but not considerably, altered view of *Sense and Sensibility* is that of Andrew Wright: "What the book most significantly illustrates is that both Sense and Sensibility are desirable, indeed necessary, for a whole life: but they are mutually exclusive."[13] For Wright "the 'lesson' of the book is that neither mode is adequate, each contradicts the other—and there is no happy medium."[14] To read the novel the way Mudrick and Wright do is to read it, I think, in the very same way that "Love and Freindship" (sic) asks to be read.

Jane Austen's first extended treatment of sensibility in "Love and Freindship" was a hilarious flirtation with the ridiculous. The letters of Laura are addressed to Marianne and they contain "a regular detail of the Misfortunes and Adventures"[15] of her life—the life of a woman of Sensibility. "Love and Freindship" is a grotesque account of the influence of sensibility on people's lives. It is grotesque because none of the characters of sensibility—Laura or Edward, August or Sophia, Philander or Gustavus—has any intelligence at all. Precisely because it is so grotesque, "Love and Freindship" shows, by exaggerating them,

the dangers of an ungoverned sensibility. In this little piece
"Sensibility" makes everything right. A few instances will
serve to illustrate its supremacy.

Edward happens in upon Laura and her parents and tells them
the story of his misfortune:

> "My Father, seduced by the false glare of Fortune and the Deluding
> Pomp of Title, insisted on my giving my hand to Lady Dorothea.
> No never exclaimed I. Lady Dorothea is lovely and Engaging; I
> prefer no woman to her; but know Sir, that I scorn to marry her in
> compliance with your Wishes. No! Never shall it be said that I
> obliged my Father."
>
> We all admired the noble Manliness of his reply. He continued.
>
> Sir Edward was surprized; he had perhaps little expected to meet
> with so spirited an opposition to his will. 'Where, Edward in the
> name of wonder (said he) did you pick up this unmeaning gibberish?
> You have been studying Novels I suspect.' I scorned to answer: it
> would have been beneath my dignity. I mounted my Horse and
> followed by my faithful William set forwards for my Aunts" (81).

Edward, of course, marries Laura the same night that he meets
her, and away they go together only to meet, accidentally, Lady
Dorothea:

> I soon perceived that tho' Lovely and Elegant in her Person and tho'
> Easy and Polite in her Address, she was of that Inferior order of
> Beings with regard to Delicate Feeling, tender Sentiments, and
> refined Sensibility, of which Augusta was one.
>
> She staid but half an hour and neither in the Course of her Visit,
> confided to me any of her secret thoughts, nor requested me to
> confide in her, any of Mine. You will easily imagine therefore my
> Dear Marianne that I could not feel any ardent affection or very
> sincere Attachment for Lady Dorothea (84).

Sophia, the wife of Edward's friend Augustus, is more to Laura's
liking:

> She was all Sensibility and Feeling. We flew into each others arms
> and after having exchanged vows of mutual Freindship [sic] for the
> rest of our Lives, instantly unfolded to each other the most inward
> secrets of our Hearts. (85).

Edward and Laura stay on with their friends and find almost
unutterable bliss:

> In the society of my Edward and this Amiable Pair, I passed the
> happiest moments of my Life; Our time was most delightfully
> spent, in mutual Protestations of Freindship, and in vows of
> unalterable Love, in which we were secure from being interrupted,
> by intruding and disagreable [sic] Visitors, as Augustus and Sophia had
> on their first Entrance in the Neighbourhood, taken due care to
> inform the surrounding Families, that as their Happiness centered
> wholly in themselves, they wished no other society (87).

Fortunately for Edward and Laura, Augustus has enough money
for everyone:

> They had been married but a few months when our visit to them
> commenced during which time they had been amply supported by a
> considerable sum of Money which Augustus had gracefully pur-
> loined from his unworthy father's Escritoire, a few days before his
> union with Sophia (88).

The story runs on in this madcap manner, but we need pursue it
no further. These few instances clearly indicate that a person of
unadulterated sensibility has, as Edward's treatment of his
father shows, no regard for authority, even when its requests are
reasonable. Nor is a person of pure sensibility able to make a
right judgment: Laura rejects Dorothea and accepts Sophia.
Moreover, people of intense sensibility live in a universe all
their own: "their happiness centered wholly in themselves";
and actions that the world may consider criminal, when done
with sensibility—"gracefully purloined"—by a person of sensibility to support a life of sensibility are perfectly justified.
All this, of course, is grotesque and a caricature of sensibility

in *Sense and Sensibility*, but it is well to note that the characteristics of sensibility outlined above do appear in a subdued
fashion in Marianne at the beginning of *Sense and Sensibility*. She
is insensible to the authority of custom, makes poor judgments,
disregards the world, and displays a morality of sensibility. It is the
business of the novel to show the gradual enlightenment of
Marianne's sensibility, and the dynamism of that enlightenment
requires a finesse in reading that the static "Love and Freindship"
dares not ask.

This is certainly the view of Walton Litz, who finds "obvious
attempts in *Sense and Sensibility* to mediate between reason and
feeling, social conventions and individual passion."[16] But for
Litz the attempt is without success:

> The novel threatens at every turn to resolve itself into unrealistic
> antitheses, and we must finally conclude that in providing Marianne
> with a choice between Willoughby's weakness and Colonel Bran-
> don's "flannel waistcoat" Jane Austen was confessing her inability
> to transform the conventions inherited from other writers and
> embodied in the novel's original versions.[17]

Ian Watt insists that the reader

> abandon any attempt to view the book as based on an unqualified and
> diametrical opposition between sense and sensibility, and see instead
> that Jane Austen requires us to make much more complex dis-
> criminations between the two terms.[18]

Howard Babb takes the same tack:

> The novel contends that the individual can morally engage himself
> in the social organism, of which he is necessarily a part, only
> when he achieves an appropriate balance between sense and
> feeling. Both are necessary: sense to formulate his relation with
> society, feeling to vitalize it. . . . For *Sense and Sensibility* finally
> insists—though awkwardly at moments—on Marianne's capacity
> to reason and on Elinor's capacity to feel in making decisions.[19]

This conclusion of Babb's is not unlike Watt's final judgment on the novel: ". . . Despite a certain amount of awkwardly obtrusive manipulation, Jane Austen nevertheless brought off her supreme coup as a matchmaker, and triumphantly introduced Sense to Sensibility."[20]

My own notion of *Sense and Sensibility* is not only that Watt and Babb are correct, but that they have not gone quite far enough in their claims for *Sense and Sensibility*. I want to show in the following pages how the very structure of the novel attempts to engage and develop the total personalities of Elinor and Marianne by presenting them with a series of mysteries that must be solved. The novel proposes to Marianne tests of intellectual, moral, and emotional exertion which join her sensibility to sense at the same time that they and other tasks engage the sensibility of Elinor, whose sense, of course, is seldom in doubt. Perhaps in this discussion of the plot of *Sense and Sensibility* some rationale can also be provided for that obvious awkwardness all agree on— Colonel Brandon's revelation—and for some lesser gaucheries as well.

Edward Ferrars is the first mysterious character to appear in *Sense and Sensibility*. He is introduced as "a gentlemanlike and pleasing young man,"[21] but not as a dashing hero.

> Edward Ferrars was not recommended to their good opinion by any particular graces of person or address. He was not handsome, and his manners required intimacy to make them pleasing. He was too diffident to do justice to himself; but when his natural shyness was overcome, his behaviour gave every indication of an open affectionate heart (15).

Marianne and Elinor disagree on Edward's merits, but the younger sister is willing to think anew when the circumstances are right: "I shall very soon think him handsome, Elinor, if I do not now. When you tell me to love him as a brother, I shall no more see imperfection in his face, than I now do in his heart"

(20–21). But Elinor is by no means sure of Edward's love for her: "sometimes, for a few painful minutes, she believed it to be no more than friendship" (22); therefore, she is careful not to allow Marianne to hope too much: " 'I do not attempt to deny,' said she, 'that I think very highly of him—that I greatly esteem, that I like him' " (21). Although Marianne abhors the words "like" and "esteem," Elinor holds to them because there is something mysterious about Edward: "There was at times a want of spirits about him which, if it did not denote indifference, spoke a something almost as unpromising" (22). Elinor, consequently, "was far from depending on that result of his preference of her, which her mother and sister still considered as certain" (22). Not long afterward, Marianne gives voice to a mounting perplexity when she recalls to her mother their parting from Edward at Norland:

> ". . . In Edward's farewell there was no distinction between Elinor and me: it was the good wishes of an affectionate brother to both. Twice did I leave them purposely together in the course of the last morning, and each time did he most unaccountably follow me out of the room . . ." (39).

When Edward arrives for a visit at Barton cottage, he in no way reduces the air of mystery surrounding him:

> He was confused, seemed scarcely sensible of pleasure in seeing them, looked neither rapturous nor gay, said little but what was forced from him by questions, and distinguished Elinor by no mark of affection (87).

Edward's conduct disturbs Elinor more than ever: "His coldness and reserve mortified her severely; she was vexed and half angry . . ." (89). He relapses from moments of gaiety into periods of melancholy: "His gravity and thoughtfulness returned on him in their fullest extent—and he sat for some time silent and dull" (95). Again: "Elinor saw, with great uneasiness, the low spirits of her friend. His visit afforded her but a very partial satisfaction, while his own enjoyment in it appeared so imperfect. It was evident that he was unhappy . . ." (96). Finally:

> Edward remained a week at the cottage; he was earnestly pressed by Mrs. Dashwood to stay longer; but as if he were bent only on self-mortification, he seemed resolved to be gone when his enjoyment among his friends was at the height. His spirits, during the last two or three days, though still very unequal, were greatly improved—he grew more and more partial to the house and environs—never spoke of going away without a sigh—declared his time to be wholly disengaged—even doubted to what place he should go when he left them—but still, go he must (101).

Elinor's greater acquaintance with Edward has given her no clue to the mystery. His being in Devonshire two weeks before visiting them, his wearing a ring "with a plait of hair in the centre," his periods of depression, his reserved conduct towards her, and his leaving for no apparent reason just when he is beginning to enjoy himself: all these things confuse and distress Elinor. She can provide no reasonable explanation for his conduct. She can allow herself no reasonable expectation of an imminent proposal of marriage from Edward. She can only prevent herself by reasonable exertion[22] "from appearing to suffer more than what all her family suffered on his going away":

> Elinor sat down to her drawing-table as soon as he was out of the house, busily employed herself the whole day, neither sought nor avoided the mention of his name, appeared to interest herself almost as much as ever in the general concerns of the family, and if, by this conduct, she did not lessen her own grief, it was at least prevented from unnecessary increase, and her mother and sisters were spared much solicitude on her account (104).

Elinor puts in practice a Johnsonian principle enunciated in *The Rambler*, no. 47: "The safe and general antidote against sorrow, is employment."

The second man of mystery to appear in *Sense and Sensibility* is Colonel Brandon, and the symptoms of mystery in him are the same as they are in Edward: an inexplicable melancholy and a sudden and unexplained departure. The narrator introduces Brandon with an air of impartiality:

> He was silent and grave. His appearance however was not un-unpleasing, in spite of his being in the opinion of Marianne and Margaret an absolute old bachelor, for he was on the wrong side of five and thirty; but though his face was not handsome his coun-tenance was sensible, and his address was particularly gentleman-like (34).

When time allows Elinor to observe Brandon more closely, he is seen to close ranks with Edward as a mysterious individual:

> She liked him—in spite of his gravity and reserve, she beheld in him an object of interest. His manners, though serious, were mild; and his reserve appeared rather the result of some oppression of spirits, than of any natural gloominess of temper. Sir John had dropt hints of past injuries and disappointments, which justified her belief of his being an unfortunate man, and she regarded him with respect and compassion (50).

Marianne, who found Edward wanting in "spirit" and "real taste" (17),[23] announces that Brandon "has neither genius, taste, nor spirit" (51). Marianne places Edward and the Colonel in the same category; Jane Austen does the same when she causes him to leave Barton Park on the spur of the moment:

> While they were at breakfast the letters were brought in. Among the rest there was one for Colonel Brandon;—he took it, looked at the direction, changed colour, and immediately left the room.
> "What is the matter with Brandon?" said Sir John. Nobody could tell (63).

Willoughby is introduced into *Sense and Sensibility* in a manner
that announces him the antithesis of Ferrars and Brandon.

> A gentleman carrying a gun, with two pointers playing round him,
> was passing up the hill and within a few yards of Marianne, when
> her accident happened. He put down his gun and ran to her assis-
> tance. She had raised herself from the ground, but her foot had
> been twisted in the fall, and she was scarcely able to stand. The
> gentleman offered his services, and perceiving that her modesty
> declined what her situation rendered necessary, took her up in his
> arms without farther delay, and carried her down the hill. Then
> passing through the garden, the gate of which had been left open
> by Margaret, he bore her directly into the house, whither Margaret
> was just arrived, and quitted not his hold till he had seated her in a
> chair in the parlour (42).

The girl in distress, the countryside, the pointers, the gun, the
gallantry, the quick and decisive action: all announce a man
neither diffident nor melancholy. Willoughby is soon seen to be
the man Marianne earlier demanded: "I could not be happy with
a man whose taste did not in every point coincide with my own.
He must enter into all my feelings; the same books, the same
music must charm us both" (17):

> The same books, the same passages were idolized by each—or if
> any difference appeared, any objection arose, it lasted no longer
> than till the force of her arguments and the brightness of her eyes
> could be displayed. He acquiesced in all her decisions, caught all
> her enthusiasm; and long before his visit concluded, they conversed
> with the familiarity of a long-established acquaintance (47).

To Marianne, Willoughby is perfect; to Elinor, however, he is
less than a paragon:

> . . . Elinor saw nothing to censure in him but a propensity, in
> which he strongly resembled and peculiarly delighted her sister, of
> saying too much what he thought on every occasion, without atten-
> tion to persons or circumstances. In hastily forming and giving his

opinion of other people, in sacrificing general politeness to the
enjoyment of undivided attention where his heart was engaged, and
slighting too easily the forms of worldly propriety, he displayed a
want of caution which Elinor could not approve, in spite of all that
he and Marianne could say in its support (48–49).

This readiness on Willoughby's part to be candid on all subjects
is the very thing that makes him mysterious, because on one
subject he refuses to be frank. Willoughby in every way appears
to love Marianne: he offers her one of his horses as her own, he
addresses her "by her christian name alone," he accepts from
her a lock of hair, he takes her on a tour of Allenham, which he
expects to inherit. To Elinor these actions bespeak "an intimacy
so decided, a meaning so direct, as marked a perfect agreement
between them" (60). To Elinor and her mother and to friends
of the Dashwoods, the intimacy of Marianne and Willoughby
can only mean that they are engaged. But this is exactly the point
of mystery: Elinor "doubted not of their being engaged to each
other; and the belief of it created no other surprise, than that
she, or any of their friends, should be left by tempers so frank,
to discover it by accident" (60). But the silence of the outspoken
couple persists and the dilemma remains until Willoughby,
suddenly and unexpectedly, does what Ferrars and Brandon did
before him: he leaves without a reasonable explanation.

> Willoughby may undoubtedly have very sufficient reasons for his
> conduct [Elinor tells her mother], and I will hope that he has. But
> it would have been more like Willoughby to acknowledge them at
> once. Secrecy may be advisable; but I still cannot help wondering
> at its being practiced by him (79).

Willoughby quickly becomes the third man of mystery in *Sense
and Sensibility*, and Marianne just as quickly becomes, in Dr.
Johnson's words, one of those who have

> suffered all sensibility of pleasure to be destroyed by a single blow,
> have given up for ever the hopes of substituting any other object

in the room of that which they lament, resigned their lives to gloom and despondence, and worn themselves out in unavailing misery.[24]

The two marriages that end *Sense and Sensibility* depend on the solution of these three mysteries that begin it. The subsequent action of the novel is directed to the removal of the mystery that shrouds the conduct of Ferrars, Brandon, and Willoughby and to the alleviation of the visible depression of spirits noted in Edward and Colonel Brandon. To these ends the plot moves carefully through a series of revelations and a set of crises to the marriages of Edward and Elinor, Brandon and Marianne.

The first revelation is made by Lucy Steele, who tells Elinor in confidence that she has been engaged to Edward Ferrars for four years. This revelation makes perfectly clear why Edward is reserved in manners and depressed in spirits: he is the victim of a conflict between love and honor. He loves Elinor but his honor is engaged to Lucy. Elinor is sure that Edward loves her:

> His affection was all her own. She could not be deceived in that. Her mother, sisters, Fanny, all had been conscious of his regard for her at Norland; it was not an illusion of her own vanity. He certainly loved her (139–40).

Moreover, Lucy Steele does not love Edward:

> Edward was not only without affection for the person who was to be his wife, but . . . he had not even the chance of being tolerably happy in marriage, which sincere affection on *her* side would have given, for self-interest alone could induce a woman to keep a man to an engagement, of which she seemed so thoroughly aware that he was weary (151).

Under these circumstances one can only wonder why Edward does not terminate the engagement. Is honor only a meaningless adherence to social form, as one critic has suggested?[25] Another revelation is needed to answer this question.

The second revelation of the novel comes in Willoughby's letter to Marianne:

> My esteem for your whole family is very sincere; but if I have been
> so unfortunate as to give rise to a belief of more than I felt, or meant
> to express, I shall reproach myself for not having been more guarded
> in my professions of that esteem. That I should ever have meant more
> you will allow to be impossible, when you understand that my
> affections have been long engaged elsewhere, and it will not be
> many weeks, I believe, before this engagement is fulfilled. It is
> with great regret that I obey your commands of returning the
> letters, with which I have been honoured from you, and the lock
> of hair, which you so obligingly bestowed on me (183).

Marianne is now in a situation that parallels Elinor's: both
sisters love men who are engaged to other women. Also, just as
Edward's engagement is perplexing, so too is Willoughby's:
both require yet another revelation to make sense. These first
revelations have only made Edward and Willoughby more mysterious than ever. The sincere *love* of Willoughby for Marianne
gives the lie especially to his simple profession of *esteem*.

The third revelation is Brandon's to Elinor. It explains both his
abrupt departure from Barton and his prevailing melancholy.
The letter that reached him at Barton was from his ward, Eliza
Williams; she had run away, become pregnant, and found herself
in want of his help. Moreover, Willoughby is to blame for Eliza's
condition: "Little did Mr. Willoughby imagine, I suppose,
when his looks censured me for incivility in breaking up the
party, that I was called away to the relief of one, whom he had
made poor and miserable . . ." (209). In addition to this, Brandon
explains that, from their first meeting, Marianne reminded him
of the young lady who was his first love, who unhappily married
his brother and who subsequently was divorced from her husband,
led a dissolute life, gave birth to Eliza Williams, and almost
literally died in his arms. The fate of his first love and of her
daughter and the striking resemblance of Marianne's person and
situation to both explain Brandon's initial, continued, and
increased right to be less than happy.

The next revelation is Willoughby's; it too is made to Elinor. It comes when Marianne is seriously ill because of physical debilitation brought on by emotional anguish at Willoughby's desertion. Clearly, when Willoughby arrives at Cleveland, Marianne, Brandon's second love, threatens to repeat the fate of his first. Willoughby explains to Elinor that his abrupt departure from Devonshire followed on his aunt's discovery of his seduction and desertion of Eliza Williams, and that his cold-blooded letter to Marianne in London attested only to an unflagging devotion to his wife's wealth.

> "And in short—what do you think of my wife's style of letter-writing?—delicate—tender—truly feminine—was it not?"
> "Your wife!—The letter was in your own handwriting."
> "Yes, but I had only the credit of servilely copying such sentences as I was ashamed to put my name to" (328).

Thus the pressure of complex motivation, while not excusing it, mitigates Willoughby's conduct and makes more realistic the relationship between the warmth of his person and the coldness of his deeds. As Marianne wished, Willoughby's heart is made known and she announces herself "perfectly satisfied." She even finds that "I never could have been happy with him, after knowing . . . all this.—I should have had no confidence, no esteem" (350). The mystery of Willoughby ends with this revelation, and the intellectual and moral—if not the emotional —satisfaction of Marianne is complete.

Elinor's satisfaction is more immediately total when Edward Ferrars arrives at Barton cottage with the final revelation that Lucy has married his brother Robert. Edward reveals that he had been true to his engagement to Lucy because he believed her in love with him until the moment he received a letter from her signed "Lucy Ferrars":

> . . . Till her last letter reached him, he had always believed her to be a well-disposed, good-hearted girl, and thoroughly attached to

himself. Nothing but such a persuasion could have prevented his
putting an end to an engagement, which, long before the discovery
of it laid him open to his mother's anger, had been a continual
source of disquiet and regret to him.

"I thought it my duty," said he, "independent of my feelings,
to give her the option of continuing the engagement or not, when
I was renounced by my mother, and stood to all appearance without
a friend in the world to assist me. In such a situation as that, where
there seemed nothing to tempt the avarice or the vanity of any
living creature, how could I suppose, when she so earnestly, so
warmly insisted on sharing my fate, whatever it might be, that
anything but the most disinterested affection was her inducement?"
(367).

Edward's honor is revealed as no meaningless social form. He
believed that Lucy Steele loved him and depended on him and
that he had no right to dissolve an engagement that he freely
entered into when it was to his convenience and her detriment.
Elinor, with Marianne, can now say, "I am perfectly satisfied."

The mystery men gradually become less mysterious as the
novel develops. The more Elinor hears, the more she understands and sympathizes: she even feels a "pang for Willoughby."
The better she understands Marianne, the better Marianne is
able to assess her own emotional attachments. An understanding
of the truth becomes the basis of the affective relationships that
Elinor and Marianne establish with Edward and Brandon before
the novel ends. It is significant, too, that Marianne establishes an
emphatic relationship with Elinor and becomes like her sister
more selfless and sympathetic. The parallel structure of incidents in the novel serves the cause of empathy. Elinor falls in
love with Edward; Marianne with Willoughby. Elinor learns
Edward is engaged; Marianne learns Willoughby is soon to be
married; Elinor suffers from her discovery; Marianne from her
jilting. Elinor marries Edward; Marianne, Brandon. When
Edward's engagement to Lucy is announced, Marianne learns

that her sister has been suffering in the exact manner that she herself has, and when she learns that Elinor's feelings for Edward are as strong as her own for Willoughby, Marianne achieves her moment of insight:

> "Oh! Elinor," she cried, "you have made me hate myself for ever. —How barbarous have I been to you!—you, who have been my only comfort, who have borne with me in all my misery, who have seemed to be only suffering for me!—Is this my gratitude!—Is this the only return I can make you?—Because your merit cries out upon myself, I have been trying to do it away" (264).

Marianne, through understanding and empathy, becomes more like Elinor and, indeed, more like Brandon too. She detaches herself from an alignment with Willoughby and Lucy Steele and becomes more like her sister and her lover.

The distinction between the two groups can be established if one notes the selfishness of the former and the selflessness of the latter. Lucy Steele stands firmly behind Edward's depression and melancholy. But even before Elinor knows this she is quick to see through Lucy's character:

> Elinor saw, and pitied her for, the neglect of abilities which education might have rendered so respectable; but she saw, with less tenderness of feeling, the thorough want of delicacy, of rectitude, and integrity of mind, which her attentions, her assiduities, her flatteries at the Park betrayed; and she could have no lasting satisfaction in the company of a person who joined insincerity with ignorance; whose want of instruction prevented their meeting in conversation on terms of equality; and whose conduct toward others, made every shew of attention and deference towards herself perfectly valueless (127).

After she knows about Lucy's engagement to Edward, Elinor realizes that Lucy, as we have seen, is maintaining it in spite of Edward's disaffection and telling her about it because she is jealous of Elinor— it "was told me," Elinor remarks to Marianne, "as I thought, with triumph" (263). After Edward and Elinor are engaged, she explains Lucy's conduct to him quite accurately:

> ". . . she lost nothing by continuing the engagement, for she has proved that it fettered neither her inclination nor her actions. The connection was certainly a respectable one, and probably gained her consideration among her friends; and, if nothing more advantageous occurred, it would be better for her to marry *you* than be single" (367).

Lucy Steele, as her name indicates, is a luminously cold, hard individual. She is a creature of pure economic opportunity. Lucy is the more intelligent counterpart of John Dashwood, for both are convinced that marriages are made in the credit columns of bank books. Lucy is cold reason operating for cold cash and her reward for perseverance is Robert Ferrars, who is wealthy enough to be fastidious about toothpick cases.

Willoughby stands partly behind the depression of Brandon and wholly behind the cruel suffering of Marianne. He is a civilized emotional cannibal who devours those who satisfy his appetite: first Eliza Williams then Marianne Dashwood. He is a hunter caught in his own trap, however; for the seduction of Eliza costs him the good will of Mrs. Smith and his trifling with Marianne costs him his heart. Willoughby's is not the cold selfishness of Lucy, of course, but hot-blooded egoism all his own. Elinor characterizes him as selfish:

> Marianne's lips quivered, and she repeated the word "Selfish?" in a tone that implied—"do you really think him selfish?"
>
> "The whole of his behaviour," replied Elinor, "from the beginning to the end of the affair, has been grounded on selfishness. It was selfishness which first made him sport with your affections; which afterwards, when his own were engaged, made him delay the confession of it, and which finally carried him from Barton. His own enjoyment, or his own ease, was, in every particular, his ruling principle" (351).

Even Willoughby's calculated marriage to Sophia Grey is made
to free him from debts that his expensive habits incurred and to
keep him in horses and dogs as he hunts his way through life. It
gives him the melancholy leisure to love Marianne for the rest
of his days: "many a rising beauty would be slighted by him in
after-days as bearing no comparison with Mrs. Brandon"
(379–380).

Willoughby dramatizes an excess of sensibility being forced to
deny itself its true object because it always answers less significant
emotional calls; whereas Lucy Steele dramatizes sense overcoming
all sensibility: she allows herself to be "fettered to a man for
whom she had not the smallest regard" (367). The reward for
the indulgence of an excess of sense and an excess of sensibility
is much the same for Lucy and Willoughby: they lose Edward
and Marianne and gain, respectively, a loveless husband and wife.

The same selfishness is not characteristic of Colonel Brandon
and Elinor, with whom Marianne finally allies herself. Brandon is
continually attentive to the needs of his friends. His one offense
against civility is his abrupt departure from Sir John Middleton's
house just before the Whitwell excursion is to begin. But, as we
later learn, Eliza Williams' welfare called him from pleasure to
duty. He is invariably kind to Marianne, regardless of how she
treats her. He is helpful to Elinor, a benefactor to Edward, and a
friend-in-need to Mrs. Dashwood.

Elinor, it is clear, picks up the burdens of propriety and
civility that her mother and Marianne drop in her path. She
carries them at moments when she is already vexed by her own
emotional burdens and by the confidences and troubles of her
acquaintances. While neither an innocent nor a saint—she lies
and she dislikes and occasionally deceives—Elinor is never
unmindful of her obligations to others. "Elinor was to be the
comforter of others in her own distresses, no less than in
theirs . . ." (261). She puts simply in one sentence, which
speaks her love and suffering for Edward, her duty to all those

close to her: "I did not love only him—and while the comfort of others was dear to me, I was glad to spare them from knowing how much I felt" (263). Elinor refuses to impose on others for herself. In the words of Laurence Connoley:

> Elinor feels strongly about the people she loves. Her efforts for self-control are not a condemnation of feeling or a denial of personal longings. They spring from a conviction that individual judgment is fallible and self-centered expectation is merely wishful thinking. Her object is the happiness of others, to which nothing is contributed by displays of anguish at disappointed hopes.[26]

Marianne's conduct, by deliberate and unmistakable contrast, is the opposite. Her whole world is Willoughby:

> When he was present she had no eyes for any one else. Every thing he did, was right. Every thing he said, was clever. If their evenings at the park were concluded with cards, he cheated himself and all the rest of the party to get her a good hand. If dancing formed the amusement of the night, they were partners for half the time; and when obliged to separate for a couple of dances, were careful to stand together and scarcely spoke a word to any body else. Such conduct made them of course most exceedingly laughed at; but ridicule could not shame, and seemed hardly to provoke them (53–54).

When Willoughby leaves her, Marianne acts as though there is no one else alive besides herself. When her world disappears, she takes upon herself a *Weltschmerz* that encompasses all in her sorrow and that systematically neglects the duty of love to her family, the responsibility of civility to her friends and acquaintances, and care for her own well-being. When Willoughby leaves, we find Marianne "not merely giving way to [violent sorrow] as a relief, but feeding and encouraging [it] as a duty" (77). Elinor's revelation of Edward's engagement to Lucy becomes a turning point in Marianne's life. She sees that Elinor has suffered all that she has and more, but has suffered without making others suffer too. Her repentance is equal to her fault: "where Marianne felt that she had injured, no reparation could be too much for her to make" (265). Marianne's near-fatal illness further introduces serious, selfless considerations into her life and she emerges from it a new woman:

". . . Whenever I looked towards the past, I saw some duty neglected, or some failing indulged. Every body seemed injured by me. The kindness, the unceasing kindness of Mrs. Jennings, I had repaid with ungrateful contempt. To the Middletons, the Palmers, the Steeles, to every common acquaintance even, I had been insolent and unjust; with an heart hardened against their merits, and a temper irritated by their very attention.—To John, to Fanny, —yes, even to them, little as they deserve, I had given less than their due. But you,—you above all, above my mother, had been wronged by me. I, and only I, knew your heart and its sorrows; yet, to what did it influence me?—not to any compassion that could benefit you or myself—Your example was before me: but to what avail?—Was I more considerate of you and your comfort? Did I imitate your forbearance, or lessen your restraints, by taking any part in those offices of general complaisance or particular gratitude which you had hitherto been left to discharge alone?—No;—not less when I knew you to be unhappy, than when I had believed you at ease, did I turn away from every exertion of duty or friendship; scarcely allowing sorrow to exist but with me, regretting only *that* heart which had deserted and wronged me, and leaving you, for whom I professed an unbounded affection, to be miserable for my sake" (346).

In her illness Marianne is cured of the selfishness that inheres in an unenlightened sensibility and she now places her strong feelings, her sensibility, in a more fitting relationship to the demands of living with others. Like Elinor, "she is convinced that reality will not be made over according to her liking by her expecting that it must, or by her resenting the fact that it will not be."[27]

Through confrontation with mystery, suffering, and love, Marianne has changed. It is undoubtedly this dynamism of character that attracts the attention of readers of *Sense and Sensibility* to Marianne. While never losing her essential identity, she evolves from the intelligent but callow girl of feeling to the intelligent and understanding woman of enlightened sensibility. If anything, in the process of change, her sensibility is affirmed, not deprecated, for it is obvious that the root of a life cannot be blighted without destroying its flower. Marianne's sensibility is not destroyed by Jane Austen; it is cultivated. It is idle to maintain that the best of Marianne has been killed by the time she marries Brandon. The best of Marianne is not her unenlightened and self-indulgent feeling: that is only the selfishness that is dramatized by her unthinking neglect of those who ruffle her sensitivity—those "whose taste did not in every point coincide with my own." In the world of the young Marianne, to whom taste is "rapturous delight," there is no allowance for differences —there is no "thou" but only an "I."[28] Her marriage to Brandon is a more than dramatic repudiation of theory for life. Indeed, the many things Marianne repents in her illness come from her early disposition to alienate and neglect those "whose taste did not in every point coincide with my own." Marianne comes to realize that there has been a great deal in her that was unlovable. But her sensibility—tempered by trial, made more feeling by suffering, and directed by understanding—brings her through magnificently in the end: "Marianne could never love by halves; and her whole heart became, in time, as much devoted to her husband, as it had once been to Willoughby" (379).

This vitalism in Marianne, this human refusal to be static, makes it difficult to concentrate on Elinor; nevertheless, Elinor is every bit as human as her sister. It is not as easy to see this, however, because Elinor's humanity is rooted in stability. Indeed, Elinor has to remain the same precisely because her sister changes. The whole of Elinor's character is revealed in the stability required to allow the change in Marianne (and others) to be successful. The structure of the novel makes this clear.

Elinor is the center of *Sense and Sensibility*. The problems that Marianne creates are hers, the problems that Willoughby creates are hers, also the problems that Lucy and Edward create are hers. Elinor is placed between contending factions and must deal with the problems of each of them. Jane Austen directs our attention to Elinor and her juggling of confidences and duties. Elinor keeps the reader in a state of suspense, pressing him to the point where he fears that she will drop some hitherto delicately handled reality and ruin her adept and intriguing performance. Keeping everything in the air requires a skillful handling of each problem with honor and with sense, so if Elinor pales as a woman of feeling in comparison with Marianne, it is simply because she must do so many things while Marianne is doing only one.

Now what are the circumstances under which Elinor works? She loves Edward, is convinced he loves her, and cannot understand why he acts as he does. Lucy Steele tells her why, but requires Elinor tell no one else. Consequently, Elinor must suffer her own disappointment and Lucy's jealousy in silence, as she later tells Marianne:

> ". . . For four months, Marianne, I have had all this hanging on my mind, without being at liberty to speak of it to a single creature. . . . It was told me,—it was in a manner forced on me by the very person herself, whose prior engagement ruined all my prospects; and told me, as I thought, with triumph . . ." (263).

Marianne is jilted by Willoughby, and Elinor must see to it that her sister does not go completely to pieces: she is to Marianne "my nurse, my friend, my sister!—You who had seen all the fretful selfishness of my latter days; who had known all the murmurings of my heart" (346). When Marianne accepts Mrs. Jennings' invitation to spend the winter in London, she so neglects her obligations that Elinor is forced to take "immediate posses-

sion of the post of civility'' (160). When Colonel Brandon
reveals Willoughby's seduction of Eliza Williams, Elinor is
entrusted with the delicate task of choosing the time and circumstances to repeat the news to her suffering sister. And
Willoughby's desire not to be more ill-thought of than circumstances require, brings him to Elinor

> ''. . . to open my heart to you, and by convincing you, that though
> I have been always a blockhead, I have not been always a rascal,
> to obtain something like forgiveness from Ma—from your sister''
> (319).

So to Elinor is committed the task of making Willoughby's heart
known to Marianne. Even Colonel Brandon's solicitude for
Edward Ferrars, which moves him to give Edward the Delaford
living, confers on Elinor the unenviable task of telling the man
she loves that he can now marry the woman he is engaged to.
If Atlas turned to stone because he had to hold up the world, it is
no wonder that Elinor, whose sense and judgment are forever
engaged in the service of others, may occasionally seem a bit
hard.

But, of course, Elinor is filled with feeling: she feels for herself, for Edward, for Marianne, for Brandon, for Willoughby, for
her mother, and for her acquaintances. But the fact that she feels
deeply and suffers much—''for four months, Marianne, I have
had all this hanging on my mind''—does not permit Elinor to
forget those with whom she lives: ''I owed it to my family and
friends, not to create in them a solicitude about me . . .'' (263).[29]
The world is too real to do away with by creating one of her own.
She has ''a better knowledge of mankind'' (261) than to believe
that the many must be sacrificed to the one.

The euphoria of young love is a final testimony to Elinor's
deep feeling for Edward and a revelation of the same sensibility
that quietly contained so much anguish throughout the novel.

Edward was now fixed at the cottage at least for a week;—for whatever other claims might be made on him, it was impossible that less than a week should be given up to the enjoyment of Elinor's company, or suffice to say half that was to be said of the past, the present, and the future;—for though a very few hours spent in the hard labour of incessant talking will dispatch more subjects than can really be in common between any two rational creatures, yet with lovers it is different. Between *them* no subject is finished, no communication is even made, till it has been made at least twenty times over (363–364).

Elinor's is a sensibility as real as Marianne's and in fact is a model of the enlightened selflessness that Marianne makes her own by the novel's end. The ultimately significant difference between Elinor and Marianne is not so much that between sense and sensibility as the difference between stasis and dynamism in a drama of feeling.

Sense and Sensibility is clearly not an endorsement of one kind of fragmented existence—that of sense—in preference to another kind of fragmented existence—that of sensibility. It is a novel about the reality of sense and sensibility being integral to every life that is meaningfully human, and it is about the necessity of sense and sensibility blending harmoniously to make life meaningful. Neither one must be allowed so exclusive a domination over a person that his life becomes less than truly human. From beginning to end the novel makes this clear by creating antithetical situations which show that actions taken for sense alone or for sensibility alone are unsatisfactory. Indeed, at the very beginning of *Sense and Sensibility* the cause of very real problems is shown to reside both in the actions of Mr. Henry Dashwood's uncle and in those of the John Dashwoods.

Mr. Henry Dashwood's uncle, through a caprice of sensibility, instead of leaving Norland without entail to his nephew, required it to go to Henry's son, John, when his father died. But "Mr. Dashwood had wished it more for the sake of his wife and daughters than for himself or his son" (4). "The son . . . was amply provided for by the fortune of his mother, which had been large, and . . . by his own marriage . . .'' (3). However, the daughters' "fortune, independent of what might arise to them from their father's inheriting that property, could be but small'' (3–4). Nevertheless,

> the whole was tied up for the benefit of this child [John Dashwood's son], who, in occasional visits with his father and mother at Norland, had so far gained on the affections of his uncle, by such attractions as are by no means unusual in children of two or three years old; an imperfect articulation, an earnest desire of having his own way, many cunning tricks, and a great deal of noise, as to outweigh all the value of all the attention which, for years, he had received from his niece and her daughters (4).

The foolish sensibility of their grand uncle seriously hurts Elinor, Marianne, and Margaret. The equally foolish sense of Mr. and Mrs. John Dashwood adds to the injury. In the irrepressible second chapter, John Dashwood resolves to carry out "my father's last request to me" and "assist his widow and daughters" (9). He proposes to give each of the girls a thousand pounds. His wife objects: "To take three thousand pounds from the fortune of their dear little boy, would be impoverishing him to the most dreadful degree" (8). He then proposes to give each of his sisters five hundred pounds. Fanny will not hear of it: ". . . It strikes me they can want no addition at all" (10). Perhaps an annuity to the mother from which the sisters will benefit might be better, thinks John. "But then if Mrs. Dashwood should live fifteen years, we shall be completely taken in," observes the mathematical Fanny (10). "A present of fifty pounds, now and then," may be better (11). "I am convinced within myself that your father had no idea of your giving them any money at all," reasons his wife (12). Even "some little present of furniture" when they move is ruled out (12). "Acts of assistance and kindness" (11) are approved, though, because they are less expensive. Finally, in an ironic reversal, Fanny regrets that when Mrs. Dashwood and her daughters move they will take "all the china, plate, and linen" with them—especially that "set of breakfast china [which] is twice as handsome as what belongs to this house" (13).

The chapter is a delightful *tour de force* that dramatizes the reduction of reasonable conduct to selfishness. Reflecting on Henry Dashwood's last request of his son, Fanny says:

> "The assistance he thought of, I dare say, was only such as might be *reasonably* expected of you; for instance, such as looking out for a comfortable small house for them, helping them move their things, and sending presents of fish and game, and so forth, whenever they are in season. I'll lay my life that he meant nothing farther; indeed it would be very strange and *unreasonable* if he did" (12; italics added).

The flicker of sensibility in John Dashwood is snuffed out by sense reduced to economy in his wife. So at the very beginning of *Sense and Sensibility*, in the first and second chapters, the un-enlightened sensibility of the Dashwoods' uncle and the unfeeling sense of John and his wife, combine to squeeze mother and daughters out of their house at Norland and to present Elinor and Marianne to the world some thousands of pounds poorer than even the most affectionate of suitors would like. Indeed, Willoughby ultimately rejects Marianne because her fortune is not large enough, and Edward has a falling out with his mother because of Elinor's lack of consequence. Sense without sensibility, sensibility devoid of sense can only cause trouble. Surely the title of the novel uses the word *and* conjunctively, not otherwise: to be a whole person, one must have sensibility enlightened by sense.

The plot of the novel shows this to be true. The plot, which bears down so heavily on mystery, controls the development of human wholeness. Marianne learns that one cannot be indifferent to mystery by spinning out subjective solutions to problems that have extra-personal and objective causes. She becomes convinced that reality will not be made over according to her liking and expectation simply because she is Marianne. She learns that one must be careful to know before he judges and to judge before he acts. The fact that Elinor is aware of the world outside herself and her family and of the actions that indicate and symbolize meanings to that world, gives her the advantage of her sister. Elinor's confrontation with mystery and gradual understanding of the mystery behind each of the principal male characters, enable her to judge and act reasonably even though she feels deeply her own and Marianne's involvement in the course of events. Elinor consistently presents an ideal of human action in the world as Jane Austen dramatizes it. And Marianne moves toward that ideal. Significantly, at the end of the novel, Marianne's sensibility is strengthened by sense, and Elinor, who had previously been unable to display her deep feeling, now does so.

> . . . Jane Austen shows Elinor nearly overcome by joyful emotion when she hears that Edward Ferrars is, after all, going to be free to marry her: she "almost ran out of the room, and as soon as the door was closed, burst into tears of joy."[30]

Also, Edward, who had been so depressed by his engagement to Lucy is now overjoyed to make Elinor his fiancée. And Brandon, whose life had long been melancholy, rejoices in Marianne: "her regard and her society restored his mind to animation, and his spirits to cheerfulness" (379). As Jane Austen rounds out the novel, then, she not only provides solutions to the basically intellectual problems the mysteries present, but also to the basically emotional manifestations of the problems found in the melancholy of Ferrars and Brandon. She rounds out the novel, in short, by insisting on solutions of sense *and* sensibility.

Furthermore, the direction of the action insists on such a solution by asking of both sisters a perception of the relationship between the realities signified by the words "love" and "esteem." These words are introduced into *Sense and Sensibility* in a discussion between Elinor and her mother.

> "It is enough," said she; "to say that he [Edward] is unlike Fanny is enough. It implies every thing amiable. I love him already."
> "I think you will like him," said Elinor, "when you know more of him."
> "Like him!" replied her mother with a smile. "I can feel no sentiment of approbation inferior to love."
> "You may esteem him."
> "I have never yet known what it was to separate esteem and love" (16).

Mrs. Dashwood, perhaps unknowingly, asserts the proper relationship between love and esteem. A man who is not esteemed cannot be loved. Elinor again affirms her esteem for Edward in a conversation with her sister.

> "I do not attempt to deny," said she, "that I think very highly of him—that I greatly esteem, that I like him."
> Marianne here burst forth with indignation—
> "Esteem him! Like him! Cold-hearted Elinor! Oh! worse than cold-hearted! Ashamed of being otherwise. Use those words again and I will leave the room this moment" (21).

Marianne does not perceive the niceness of Elinor's distinction here. Elinor cannot profess love for Edward because his conduct toward her has not been that of a lover. Nevertheless, Edward has always conducted himself as a gentleman, as one who deserves esteem. Even after his engagement to Lucy Steele is made known, he does not forfeit Elinor's esteem: as long as "she could *esteem* Edward as much as ever . . . her mind might be always supported" (179).

By contrast, Willoughby's conduct cannot inspire esteem. He courts Marianne without reserve and he jilts her with impunity. Colonel Brandon's revelation of Willoughby's relationship with Eliza Williams further serves to show that he is undeserving of esteem. After Marianne, who has suffered from Willoughby's rejection, discovers how Eliza has suffered from his abandonment, she asserts the impossibility of her ever having been happy as his wife:

> "I am now perfectly satisfied, I wish for no change. I never could have been happy with him, after knowing, as sooner or later I must have known, all this.—I should have had no confidence, no esteem. Nothing could have done it away to my feelings" (350).

Marianne, who can no longer esteem Willoughby, now finds it impossible to love him.

Esteem, in Johnson's definition, is "reverential regard"; it is, in Gay's words, "virtue's right alone."[31] Willoughby has forfeited all right to esteem and to the love that is consequent on it. But from the first moment we meet him, Brandon is found deserving of esteem: "He paid her [Marianne] only the compliment of attention; and she felt a respect for him on the occasion, which the others had reasonably forfeited by their shameless want of taste" (35). Though the wrong side of thirty-five, flannel waistcoats, and Willoughby's opinion turn Marianne against Brandon for a time, she eventually comes to share Elinor's "esteem for the general benevolence" of the colonel (283).

> Marianne Dashwood was born to an extraordinary fate. She was born to discover the falsehood of her own opinions, and to counteract, by her conduct, her most favourite maxims. She was born to overcome an affection formed so late in life as at seventeen, and with no sentiment superior to strong esteem and lively friendship, voluntarily to give her hand to another!—and *that* other, a man who had suffered no less than herself under the event of a former attachment, whom, two years before, she had considered too old to be married,—and who still sought the constitutional safeguard of a flannel waistcoat! (378)

And soon, since esteem and love are hard to keep apart, "lively friendship" turns to love: "her whole heart became in time, as much devoted to her husband, as it had once been to Willoughby" (379).

Brandon's revelation—to which we may now add Lucy Steele's letter—the critics, as we have seen, have found reprehensible. But Jane Austen obviously did not. Rather, she found Willoughby to be reprehensible and allowed Brandon to send a letter that would give the *coup de grâce* to Marianne's love by killing her esteem for Willoughby. The fact that Marianne could be so moved affirms a close relationship between moral and emotional responses; it affirms a wholeness in the human being. Although readers may inevitably be dissatisfied with Brandon's revelation, it enables Jane Austen to take a position on marriage not unlike that of Richardson's Harriet Byron in *Sir Charles Grandison*:

> "Love merely *personal*, that sort of love which commences between the years of fifteen and twenty; and when the extraordinary *merit* of the object is not the foundation of it, may I believe, and perhaps generally *ought* to, be subdued. But love that is founded on a merit that everybody acknowledges—I don't know what to say to the vincibility of such a love."[32]

Marianne marries a man whose "merit . . . everybody acknow-ledges." In so doing, she marries a man in his late thirties who wears flannel against the cold. For him and for her their happy marriage is the result of a second attachment. Perhaps we may finally feel that this is just a little too much humble pie for a girl with Marianne's graceful figure to eat. But if this is so, we ought at least to remember the purpose and effect of the diet: it gives a girl of strong feelings the intellectual and moral nourishment she needs to become a woman.

3

The Plot of *Pride and Prejudice*

Pride and Prejudice has long been considered a classic by the general reader,[1] but it no longer enjoys that distinction with many professional critics. To the latter, in the post-James and anti-plot era,[2] it seems too elegantly dressed in a strait jacket of form. "Exactness of symmetry," writes Mary Lascelles, ". . . carries with it one danger. The novelist's subtlety of apprehension may be numbed by this other faculty of his for imposing order on what he apprehends."[3] The question, of course, is whether this is truly the case with *Pride and Prejudice*. Has the form of the novel been preserved at the expense of the life of the characters it presents? Miss Lascelles herself objects to Darcy's letter: "The manner is right, but not the matter: so much, and such, information would hardly be volunteered by a proud and reserved man—unless under pressure from his author, anxious to get on with the story."[4] But the same proud and reserved man, we remember, rather loudly refused to dance with Elizabeth at Meryton. Did he do that on his own volition or on the author's? The difficulty of answering this question suggests the impossibility of dealing satisfactorily with the problem concerning the letter. A Darcy who could say within earshot of a young lady, "She is tolerable; but not handsome enough to tempt *me*; and I am in no humour at present to give consequence to young ladies who are slighted by other men"[5]—that same Darcy could certainly write a letter to justify *himself* when falsely accused. But even if one were disposed to admit that Darcy is inconsistent, he could find a view of character in eighteenth-century conduct books that sees such inconsistency as natural. Lady Sarah Pennington writes that "the

best men are sometimes inconsistent with themselves . . . they
may have some oddities of behaviour, some peculiarities of
temper . . . blemishes of this kind often shade the brightest
character . . ."[6] The kind of question that Darcy's letter raises is
open to endless debate. It is too much involved with too many
critical presuppositions to be satisfactorily answered. Miss
Lascelles is troubled by it; I am not.

A problem raised by Reuben Brower—and later elaborated
by Robert Liddell and Marvin Mudrick—can be more advan-
tageously dealt with. The question of esthetic fitness that he
introduces into the evaluation of *Pride and Prejudice* deserves
serious consideration. Brower writes that "as all ambiguities are
resolved and all irony is dropped, the reader feels the closing in
of a structure by its necessary end, the end implied in the crude
judgment of Darcy in the first ballroom scene."[7] It is his opinion
that after the moment at Lambton, when Elizabeth admits "a real
interest" in Darcy's welfare, *Pride and Prejudice* is "not quite the
same sort of book."[8] "Once we have reached the scenes in
which the promise of the introduction is fulfilled, the literary
design both ironic and dramatic is complete."[9] If one admits
Brower's objection to the design of *Pride and Prejudice*, he has to
decide what he can conveniently do with the last fifteen chapters
of the novel. If the promise of the introduction is fulfilled at
Lambton, these last hundred pages must be considered supererog-
atory; and with such an excrescence marring its form, *Pride and
Prejudice* will have to be considered something less than a classic.

If we turn to the Meryton ball, however, it becomes evident
that Brower's analysis of the situation is not exact. The "promise
of the introduction" has to do with more than the crude
judgment of Darcy at the ball, which Elizabeth rectifies by her
sensitive judgment of him at Lambton. The first eligible bachelor
introduced into the novel is Charles Bingley. Everything is "Mr.
Bingley" until the ball; during and after it, Bingley is as much in
the conversation of Hertfordshire as Darcy. The Meryton ball

shows Bingley finding Jane "the most beautiful creature I ever beheld" (11) and asking her "to dance a second time" (14). Attention after the ball is as much directed to the friendly relationship between Bingley and Jane as to the fractured one between Darcy and Elizabeth. Then, after Jane is taken ill, she becomes the center of attention. While she recuperates at Netherfield Park, she and Bingley cautiously reveal their affection for each other. And because Jane is there, Elizabeth comes to visit her; this gives Darcy a chance to reconsider his refusal to dance with her at the ball. Mrs. Bennet also appears on the scene, carrying all but the marriage contract to Bingley and Jane. Unless one is ready to do without much that inspires the first twelve chapters of *Pride and Prejudice*, one has to admit the importance of Jane and Bingley and see them and their relationship as integral to "the promise of the introduction." In fact, one of the main reasons that Elizabeth gives to Darcy for her refusal to marry him concerns Jane:

> ". . . Had not my own feelings decided against you, had they been indifferent, or had they even been favourable, do you think that any consideration would tempt me to accept the man, who has been the means of ruining, perhaps for ever, the happiness of a most beloved sister?" (190)

Darcy remembers this statement so well that even after Lambton, when he knows that Elizabeth's feelings are favorable toward him, he sees to it that Bingley returns to Netherfield and consequently to Jane. When Elizabeth leaves Darcy at Lambton to attend to Lydia's elopement, the strand of action concerning Bingley and Jane—which was introduced into the novel before that concerning Darcy and herself—remains to be untangled. The dramatic design of *Pride and Prejudice* under these circumstances can hardly be thought at that point to be complete.

Another fact brings out the incompleteness quite clearly too. Before Darcy can accept Elizabeth, he has to accept her family.

He has never yet entered the Bennet house at Longbourn. Also, he has still to realize that indecorum is not the specifying charac- teristic of the Bennets alone. The wonderful interference of the egregious Lady Catherine de Bourgh in his affairs has yet to make Darcy realize that his aunt's title is nothing more than a cover that keeps the skeleton in the family closet from rattling as loudly as the bumbling Mrs. Bennet. Darcy has yet to see completely through the personal-social equation that has been the cause of much of his hauteur. Lady Catherine has yet to clear his vision once and for all. The dramatic design of *Pride and Prejudice* is not complete at Lambton.

Nor is the ironic either, simply because the ironic is so com- pletely implicated in the dramatic. Irony in *Pride and Prejudice* is more totally verbal in the first half of the novel than in the second. But the verbal irony is necessary to the ambiguity that enables Darcy and Elizabeth so completely to misunderstand each other. It would be rather foolish for Jane Austen to preserve such ironic ambiguity when she is trying to solve the problems caused by it. Such verbal irony in no sense controls the design of the novel. What is normative is personal development through perception, understanding, and affection. Irony is the handmaid of such a norm, not its master.

The norm of personal development through perception, under- standing, and affection is developed by a symmetry of plot that involves a series of actions which are dramatically ironic. The plot of *Pride and Prejudice* builds to a statement of problems that arise through verbal ambiguity. Darcy comes to think that Elizabeth loves him whereas she could not care less for him because of the way she feels about his treatment of Jane and of Wickham. It is on these matters that she is brooding when Darcy comes to her at Hunsford. When he proposes to Elizabeth, she refuses him; and Darcy wants to know why he is not accepted. His request for an explanation is soon answered with three specific accusations, but Elizabeth first asks Darcy why he proposed to her at all since it was (as he said) "against your reason, and even against your character" (190). For Darcy to have proposed irrationally to Elizabeth and to have insinuated that marriage to her would injure his character was for him simply to have insulted her. But Elizabeth puts aside the proposal for a moment and taxes Darcy, first, with preventing Bingley from marrying Jane; second, with hindering Wickham from receiving the living which he claimed was his by right. Then she doubles back to include the nature of his proposal in a third charge that indicts his manners, which impress "me with the fullest belief of your arrogance, your conceit, and your selfish disdain of the feelings of others" (193). Then Darcy places an obstacle of his own in the way of their marrying. He reminds Elizabeth of the indecorous and reprehensible conduct of her family. Darcy had hesitated to propose to Elizabeth because of her family, and he now accuses her of being piqued because "your pride [had] been hurt by my honest confession of the scruples that had long prevented my forming any serious design" (192). There is no question but that at Hunsford parsonage Darcy and Elizabeth for the first time understand each other completely and unequivocally.

The first thirty-three chapters have inevitably led to this moment of passionate clarity. The conflicts and organization of these chapters make it necessary for Elizabeth to charge Darcy with bad faith and worse manners and for Darcy to indict the manners of Elizabeth's mother and father and younger sisters. The Meryton ball, which organizes much of the action and conversation until the sixth chapter, introduces two main actions into the novel. It is at the ball that the romance between Bingley and Jane begins and that Elizabeth's first unfortunate encounter with Darcy occurs: he finds her tolerable but not tempting. Chapters 7 through 12 are organized around Jane, ill but in love at Netherfield Park. There Darcy becomes attracted to Elizabeth, who does not like him at all. There Mrs. Bennet visits her daughter and shows herself a matchmaker and an enemy of Darcy. The court-

ship of Collins runs sporadically through Chapters 13 to 26
(I. 13 to II. 3),[10] which present Bingley's puzzling retreat to
London and Wickham's reports of Darcy's injustice to him.
Elizabeth becomes increasingly impatient with Darcy because
she believes that he has been unfair to Wickham, whom she likes,
and because she believes he has forced Bingley to leave Jane. At
the same time, Darcy's attraction to Elizabeth grows stronger.
Charlotte's invitation brings Elizabeth to Hunsford—Chapters
26 to 38 (II. 3 to 15)—where she sees Darcy once again, and it is
at the Collinses' parsonage that they meet in the fashion described
above. Quite clearly, *Pride and Prejudice* builds to that moment of
conflict.

Only when the four problems that have been so carefully
developed and then explicitly stated at Hunsford are solved can
the novel come to an end. The problems are not all solved by the
time Elizabeth leaves Lambton, and the dramatic irony implicit in
them is not fully released until after that point in the novel. The
dramatic and ironic design of the novel is not complete until
Darcy comes to Longbourn and proposes to Elizabeth. By the
time he does that, both he and she have matured intellectually
and emotionally as individuals and are ready for the personal
encounter of marriage. It is a great triumph of form that one
finds in the second half of *Pride and Prejudice*, and it is one of the
great delights of reading *Pride and Prejudice* to see how Jane Austen
worked out the design of the novel after Chapter 34 (II. 11) in
relation to the four problems presented at Hunsford. One might
best begin to demonstrate this position by returning to that
letter of Darcy's that Mary Lascelles so much objected to.

Darcy's letter to Elizabeth, which she receives the day following his extraordinary proposal, directs itself in detail to two of
the accusations she made against him. Because Elizabeth has
called into question Darcy's moral character, he does more than
ask her attention to his letter: "I demand it," he writes, "of
your justice" (196).

Darcy's letter explains his role in Bingley's leaving Jane, and it explains his obligations toward Wickham as well. Elizabeth learns that Darcy thought that Jane's "look and manners were open, cheerful and engaging as ever, but without any symptom of peculiar regard" for Bingley (197); she learns that he did not think he was doing Jane a personal injury by separating Bingley from her. Moreover, Bingley was courting the danger of connecting himself with a family that Darcy taxes with a "total want of propriety" (198); Elizabeth had thought that he objected to her family's lack of connections. Darcy next turns to Wickham's conduct toward himself and Georgiana, and he offers Colonel Fitzwilliam, whom Elizabeth has found likable and charming, as a corroborating witness. So she is faced with what might be a satisfactory answer to two of her objections to Darcy, namely, his treatment of Jane and of Wickham.

Elizabeth must now decide whether her opinions of Darcy's conduct or his assertions of what his conduct has been are true. Assembling the evidence and calling memory to witness, she judges that she has been in error. "Proud and repulsive as were his manners," Mr. Darcy could not be accused of being "unprincipled or unjust," "irreligious or immoral" (207).

> She grew absolutely ashamed of herself.—Of neither Darcy nor Wickham could she think, without feeling that she had been blind, partial, prejudiced, absurd.
>
> "How despicably have I acted!" she cried.—"I, who have prided myself on my discernment!—I, who have valued myself on my abilities! who have often disdained the generous candour of my sister, and gratified my vanity, in useless or blameable distrust.—How humiliating is this discovery!—Yet, how just a humiliation!—Had I been in love, I could not have been more wretchedly blind. But vanity, not love, has been my folly.—Pleased with the preference of one [Wickham], and offended by the neglect of the other [Darcy], on the very beginning of our acquaintance, I have

courted prepossession and ignorance, and driven reason away, where either were concerned. Till this moment, I never knew myself" (208).

The psychomachy is over.[11] Elizabeth has done Darcy the justice he had demanded of her.[12]

Though Elizabeth exonerates Darcy's conduct in relation to Jane and Bingley and to Wickham, she cannot excuse the manner of his proposal to her. In justice, also, she is forced to recognize in that the performance of a man made ridiculous by vanity. He was vain enough to think that his social consequence made him personally desirable. Just as vanity drove reason away in Elizabeth's case, so too has it acted in Darcy's: he proposed to Elizabeth, one remembers, against his reason. So the problem of Darcy's manners remains, as does that of the Bennets' conduct. Elizabeth and Darcy can find no satisfactory personal relationship until these two problems are solved.

At Pemberley, Elizabeth's objection to Darcy's manners disappears. When the Gardiners ask their niece if she would like to see Pemberley, the narrator relates that Elizabeth "was obliged to assume a disinclination for seeing it" (240). The party nevertheless enters Darcy's park, and Elizabeth's expectation is delightfully thwarted: "She had never seen a place for which nature had done more, or where natural beauty had been so little counteracted by an awkward taste" (245). Elizabeth had expected to find Darcy's house and park pretentious, like its owner; all that she sees, however, bespeaks nature: at Pemberley the only art is a natural art, and it configures a natural beauty unmarred by artificiality. Withindoors Elizabeth finds "less of splendor, and more real elegance" than she had anticipated (246). She meets a housekeeper "much less fine, and more civil, than she had any notion of finding" at Pemberley (246), and from her Elizabeth hears a storybook description of Fitzwilliam Darcy, whom Mrs. Reynolds had seen grow into "the best landlord, and the best master . . . that ever lived'' (249). Elizabeth also recognizes a portrait of Darcy

> with such a smile over the face, as she remembered to have some-
> times seen, when he looked at her. . . . [Now] as she stood before
> the canvas, on which he was represented, and fixed his eyes upon
> herself, she thought of his regard with a deeper sentiment of
> gratitude than it had ever raised before (250–251).

Almost surrealistically the words Elizabeth has heard and the colors and lines she has seen take life in the person of Darcy. He greets her with the warm regard the portrait pictured and shows the Gardiners that attentiveness beyond civility his housekeeper had attributed to him. The Darcy of art comes alive, asks an introduction to the Gardiners, invites Mr. Gardiner to fish in his streams, and asks Elizabeth's permission to intro-duce Georgiana to her on the following day. Darcy's manners, which were artificial and strained in Hertfordshire and Hunsford, are all naturalness at Pemberley. Elizabeth is literally charmed out of her objections to Darcy's manners by his cordial reception of herself and her aunt and uncle, and we see his acceptance of the Gardiners as proleptic of his final acceptance of the Bennet family.

Indeed, the acceptance of the Bennet family is the only obstacle of the four mentioned at Hunsford parsonage that still stands between Darcy and Elizabeth. Before Elizabeth and the Gardiners leave the Derbyshire region that obstacle becomes more formidable because Lydia elopes with Wickham, and Wick-ham is hardly Darcy's friend. Now for Darcy to make Elizabeth his wife, he will have to make Wickham his brother. Neverthe-less, Darcy goes to London and clandestinely arranges the marriage of Lydia and Wickham, and after he learns from Lady Catherine that Elizabeth refused to promise not to marry him if she were asked, he goes to Longbourn, proposes, and is accepted. His going to Longbourn and his entering the Bennet house for the first time show that he accepts the family in spite of its faults; and sitting down to dinner with Mrs. Bennet at his side, Darcy dramatically destroys the last obstacle to his and Elizabeth's love.

This very brief analysis of the plot of *Pride and Prejudice* shows a structure that is at once dynamic and ordered. Darcy, who could not propose to Elizabeth in the midst of her family, seeks her out when she is a free agent. He and she meet at Hunsford, but his social consciousness and her annoyance mar the encounter. Happily, however, they are able to speak directly and unambiguously to each other. This significant change in their relationship enables Elizabeth to state her three objections to Darcy (he has ruined Jane's relation to Bingley; he has been unjust to Wickham; he is ill-mannered and no true gentleman) and he to state his objection to her (the members of the Bennet family, save Jane and herself, act indecorously and irresponsibly). The dynamics of their confused and ironic relationship in Hertfordshire are given an orderly perspective at Hunsford. Once the truth is clear, meaningful reflection and action become possible.

This meeting at Hunsford, therefore, is the watershed chapter of *Pride and Prejudice*. At the parsonage Elizabeth gives Darcy a cataclysmic piece of information:

> "You are mistaken, Mr. Darcy, if you suppose that the mode of your declaration affected me in any other way, than as it spared me the concern which I might have felt in refusing you, had you behaved in a more gentleman-like manner" (192).

The man gently born and gently reared is told that he is not a gentleman, and this changes his life. Elizabeth's accusation hits so true that it tortures Darcy until he becomes "reasonable enough to allow" its justice (368). In Chapter 35 (II. 12) Darcy offers causes for effects when he explains Bingley's presence in London and the reason for Wickham's lies. Then, in Chapter 36 (II. 13), Elizabeth judges the causes and her attitude changes,

because she comes for the first time to know herself. From
Chapters 1 to 35 (I. 1 to II. 12) the action of *Pride and Prejudice* is
for the most part founded on appearances, and these appearances
give the lie to reality: Darcy's manners give the lie to his moral
integrity; Jane's composure, to her feelings of love; Bingley's
leaving, to his love and candor; the Bennets' ill manners, to the
worth of Jane and Elizabeth. To Chapter 36 (II. 13) *Pride
and Prejudice* is burdened with what Elizabeth calls an "incum-
brance of mystery" (227), but from that point on the novel
proceeds on truth. The truth that is suddenly revealed at
the end of the first half of *Pride and Prejudice* brings personal
realization through self-discovery to Darcy and Elizabeth. The
second half, largely unencumbered by mystery, allows them to
pursue personal realization through love and marriage. After
each learns to know himself, they learn about each other, and
seek happiness in the context of marriage and community.

But before there can be marriage in Jane Austen, there must
be friendship; and before there can be a fitting social context for a
particular marriage, there must be a general acceptance of it on a
reasonable basis. Pemberley shows Darcy and Elizabeth developing a friendship that has a clearly reasonable and deeply affective
foundation. Wickham's eloping with Lydia tests this new relationship of Darcy and Elizabeth and deepens it through empathy.
So too does Lady Catherine de Bourgh's huff-and-puff visit to
Elizabeth at Longbourn. Darcy's return with Bingley to the
Hertfordshire region confirms his and Elizabeth's love and gives it
a new impetus with Jane's acceptance of Bingley. And the
recognition of the rightness of the Darcy-Elizabeth engagement
by Mr. Bennet and Jane and Bingley is a token of its approval by
all in society who are reasonable. I want now to look at these
incidents and to show how each of them is an elaboration of one
of the four problems stated at Hunsford and to suggest how nicely
Jane Austen can turn her variations on principal themes into
dramatic harmonies.

Just as the novel proceeds by dramatization and careful modulation to moments of self-discovery, so too does it move with care and rhythm to Darcy's second proposal and Elizabeth's acceptance. Elizabeth does not simply come to Pemberley, realize what she has denied herself, and set about redressing the error by falling in love with Darcy.[13] Nor does Darcy simply decide to buy off Elizabeth's objection to him by saving the honor of her sister. By the time Elizabeth comes to Pemberley, both she and Darcy have learned something about each other, and at Pemberley they learn more. Elizabeth first sees a house and park that bespeak the taste of true gentility, then she hears about a true gentleman and sees the portrait of one. At the moment when nature and art have conspired to dispose her to see Darcy in a new way, he appears, and he is a new man. Pemberley turns into dramatic truth the rules for judging a gentleman's worth:

> It is only from the less conspicuous scenes of life, the more retired sphere of action, from the artless tenor of domestic conduct, that the real character can, with any certainty, be drawn—these, undisguised, proclaim the man; . . . the best method, therefore, to avoid the deception in this case is, to lay no stress on outward appearances, which are too often fallacious, but to take the rule of judging from the simple unpolished sentiments of those, whose dependent connexions give them an undeniable certainty—who not only see, but who hourly feel, the good or bad effects of that disposition, to which they are subjected. By this, I mean, that if a man is equally respected, esteemed, and beloved by his tenants, by his dependents and domestics . . . you may justly conclude, he has that true good nature, that real benevolence, which delights in communicating felicity, and enjoys the satisfaction it diffuses. . . .[14]

At Pemberley, Darcy's house and park provide the more retired sphere of action, Mrs. Reynolds provides the testimony of a domestic, and Elizabeth is on hand to judge from something other than first impressions. Therefore, after Darcy takes his leave of Elizabeth at Lambton, the narrator takes occasion to comment on the course of their relationship:

> If gratitude and esteem are good foundations of affection, Elizabeth's change of sentiment will be neither improbable nor faulty. But if otherwise, if the regard springing from such sources is unreasonable or unnatural, in comparison of what is so often described as arising on a first interview with its object, and even before two words have been exchanged, nothing can be said in her defence, except that she had given somewhat of a trial to the latter method, in her partiality for Wickham, and that its ill-success might perhaps authorise her to seek the other less interesting mode of attachment (279).

Three months have elapsed since we saw Darcy at Hunsford; nevertheless, Elizabeth has been constantly in view. During this three-month period she has come to understand Darcy's conduct. But by showing such a change in one of her characters, Jane Austen suggests the possibility of the same kind of change in an equally intelligent counterpart. She shows Elizabeth changing, but brings Darcy forward when his change is complete. Elizabeth, whom we have seen doing Darcy the justice he demanded of her, finds that he has done her justice as well. Her visit to Pemberley shows her return to reason to be a reflection of his, for herself as well as for the reader. The reality of the change in both—which resulted from Elizabeth's dealing honestly with his letter and Darcy's dealing honestly with her refusal of him—is now dramatized by Elizabeth's admiration of Darcy's manners, which are impeccable, and by his acceptance of Elizabeth's relatives, who are equally without fault.

Moreover, Jane Austen has not forgotten either Darcy's role in separating Jane and Bingley or Elizabeth's former admiration for Wickham. That mutual love existed between Jane and Bingley we are certain, but Bingley himself was unsure of Jane's affection. Now Darcy can be seen in exactly the same position as Bingley was in then. The Gardiners put the case succinctly:

"Of the lady's sensations they remained a little in doubt; but that the gentleman was overflowing with admiration was evident enough" (262). Darcy, who split apart doubting lovers, is now a lover and in doubt about being loved himself. There is more than poetic justice in Darcy's feeling along his pulses the meaning of Elizabeth's strong objection to his interference with Jane and Bingley. Darcy's position moves him from mere understanding to empathy. He feels with Elizabeth her objection to his actions, and those objections in light of his own case now mean a great deal more to him. Darcy's becomes an intelligent heart.

Before Elizabeth leaves the Pemberley region, she too comes to feel the justice of Darcy's strong objections to Wickham, whereas formerly she had understood only their reasonableness. When Lydia elopes with Wickham, Elizabeth and her family are made to experience the same disgrace that threatened Darcy's when Wickham planned to elope with Georgiana. The parallel misfortunes of their sisters suggest the creation of a community of feeling between Darcy and Elizabeth. Experiencing in her own family what Darcy had experienced with Wickham in his, Elizabeth understands Darcy better and soon expresses her affection for him:

> She began now to comprehend that he was exactly the man, who, in disposition and talents, would most suit her. His understanding and temper, though unlike her own, would have answered all her wishes. It was an union that must have been to the advantage of both; by her ease and liveliness, his mind might have been softened, his manners improved, and from his judgment, information, and knowledge of the world, she must have received benefit of greater importance (312).

But Elizabeth sees quite clearly that, at this time when they are so drawn to each other through understanding and gratitude and empathy, she and Darcy seem more separated than before by Lydia and Wickham's coming together.

> Had Lydia's marriage been concluded on the most honourable
> terms, it was not to be supposed that Mr. Darcy would connect
> himself with a family, where to every other objection would now
> be added, an alliance and relationship of the nearest kind with the
> man whom he so justly scorned (311).

Fortunately, however, Darcy likens Elizabeth's sister to his own.
The parallel between Lydia and Georgiana becomes complete as
Darcy settles with Wickham and saves Lydia from "irremediable
infamy" (335). And Elizabeth learns of Darcy's second encounter
with Wickham the same way she learned of his first—by letter,
this time Mrs. Gardiner's, rather than Darcy's.[15]

Darcy's motivation for his acts of kindness is not inconsistent
with his character as it is developed in the novel. His sense of
justice is clearly presented to Elizabeth in Chapter 35 (II. 12),
and the chapters that treat Elizabeth's visit at Pemberley and
Lambton make Darcy's love for her unmistakable. His sense of
justice and his love for Elizabeth lead him to rescue Lydia, as
he afterwards confesses. His acts seem completely consistent. His
return to Netherfield Park is consistent too. He took Bingley
from Netherfield by mistake; now he returns him by design.
Bingley's return and his subsequent visit to Longbourn are salts
to the faint hopes of Mrs. Bennet, who, to secure Jane a husband,
rouses herself to the good health of robust impoliteness. She
succeeds in spite of herself because the eminent good sense and
superlative dispositions of Jane and Bingley outrun her train of
contrivance. Bingley proposes, Jane accepts, Mr. Bennet
approves. Elizabeth celebrates the "happiest, wisest, most
reasonable end" (347). She sees every expectation for Jane and
Bingley's happiness

> to be rationally founded, because they had for basis the excellent
> understanding, and super-excellent disposition of Jane, and a
> general similarity of feeling and taste between her and himself
> (347-348).

These reflections of Elizabeth on the natural and reasonable foundations for the happiness of the new couple are the antithesis of Mrs. Bennet's comment to Jane: "I was sure you could not be so beautiful for nothing!" (348). Jane's own reaction terminates in a wish that Elizabeth may enjoy equal happiness, to which the younger sister replies, "Till I have your disposition, your goodness, I never can have your happiness" (350). It is interesting to note that Jane's goodness stands here as Elizabeth's model just as her candor did when Elizabeth suffered through her revaluation of Darcy after she read his letter. Jane, who appears so early in the novel and in the important role of beloved sister, has to be attended to before Elizabeth herself can find her place at Darcy's side. Jane represents an ideal that Elizabeth respects and loves so much that her reaction to other people is frequently conditioned by their reaction to Jane. This has been a pattern in *Pride and Prejudice*. The most serious charge that Elizabeth brought against Darcy was his interference with Jane's happiness. Now that happiness is complete. Darcy not only brought Bingley back but encouraged his proposal as well. It remains for Darcy to marry Elizabeth to lay to rest the last ghost of prejudice that haunts their relationship. But not without the help of his aunt.

Lady Catherine de Bourgh travels to Longbourn to claim a hereditary right to stupidity. Mrs. Bennet's obvious maneuvers are but pallid challenges to the vulgarity of an aunt who arrives with "chaise and four" to secure the marriage of her daughter to her nephew. Lady Catherine comes to Elizabeth in the name of "honour, decorum, prudence, nay, interest" (355) to order her not to marry Darcy.

It is highly amusing not only to listen to Lady Catherine argue the reasonableness of her demands but also to hear in turn Elizabeth's logical analysis demonstrate that both the premise under which Lady Catherine made her trip—if Elizabeth refused to marry Darcy, he would marry her daughter—and the arguments used to support that premise are ludicrous. Lady Catherine offends Elizabeth's good sense with rhetorical nonsense:

> "I will not be interrupted. Hear me in silence. My daughter and my nephew are formed for each other. They are descended on the maternal side, from the same noble line; and, on the father's, from respectable, honourable, and ancient, though untitled families. Their fortune on both sides is splendid. They are destined for each other by the voice of every member of their respective houses; and what is to divide them? The upstart pretentions of a young woman without family, connections, or fortune. Is this to be endured! But it must not, shall not be. If you were sensible of your own good, you would not wish to quit the sphere, in which you have been brought up" (356).

There is no mention here of compatibility of mind and disposition, no word about attraction or affection. Lady Catherine, like Mrs. Bennet, does not look upon marriage as a proposition of nature, but as one of stereotyped convention. Both women have daughters to marry: whether there is reason or love in the marriage made is a matter of no importance so long as a marriage takes place. Each recalls to mind a sentence of Dr. Johnson's:

> The miseries, indeed, which many ladies suffer under conjugal vexations are to be considered with great pity, because their husbands are often not taken by them as objects of affection, but forced upon them by authority and violence or by persuasion and importunity, equally resistless when urged by those whom they have been accustomed to reverence and obey; and it very seldom appears that those who are thus despotic in the disposal of their children pay any regard to their domestic and personal felicity, or think it so much to be inquired whether they will be happy, as whether they will be rich.[16]

Marriage is something other than the ludicrous and tragic yoking of unsuitable partners. Those who would marry, Johnson cautions, should be aware that

> marriage is the strictest tie of perpetual friendship; that there can
> be no friendship without confidence, and no confidence without
> integrity; and that he must expect to be wretched who pays to
> beauty, riches, or politeness, that regard which only virtue and
> piety can claim.[17]

This natural and reasonable basis for marriage, which Johnson
delineates to extol, has no place in the system of a Lady Catherine
or a Mrs. Bennet, because to them marriage is simply part of a
system utterly divorced from nature itself. Lady Catherine does
no more than describe the mechanism of the system when she
details family, fortune, cradle engagements, connections, and
family expectations. She dresses out in the vulgarity of irresponsible obligation what Dr. Johnson described generically as
"friendship" based on "virtue and piety." She is the victim of an
error that Johnson elsewhere warned against: a man ought to
endeavor "to distinguish nature from custom; or that which is
established because it is right from that which is right because it
is established."[18] To the reasonable person, to one who respects
nature, Lady Catherine—who holds that a thing is right only
because it is established—can only be unreasonable, and Elizabeth tells her as much:

> "Neither duty, nor honour, nor gratitude," replied Elizabeth,
> "have any possible claim on me, in the present instance. No
> principle of either, would be violated by my marriage with Mr.
> Darcy. And with regard to the resentment of his family, or the
> indignation of the world, if the former *were* excited by his marrying
> me, it would not give me one moment's concern—and the world
> in general would have too much sense to join in the scorn" (358).

Thus beaten on her own terms, Lady Catherine travels to London
to report the insolence of Elizabeth to her nephew before she
returns to Rosings. But Lady Catherine again fails because Darcy
finds her to be the insolent one. His aunt, in fact, makes Mrs.
Bennet a bit easier for Darcy to accept as a mother-in-law.

I have dwelt at some length on Lady Catherine's visit to Long-bourn because it shows her utter vulgarity and the depersonalizing pattern of life it represents. Lady Catherine shows the danger of money and position supporting a weak mind. Because Mrs. Bennet is fortunately less wealthy, she is also less a threat to the personal order of value. And Darcy realizes this. He also realizes that when he proposed to Elizabeth at Hunsford, there was some-thing of the de Bourgh in him:

> He spoke well, but there were feelings besides those of the heart to be detailed, and he was not more eloquent on the subject of tenderness than of pride. His sense of her inferiority—of its being a degradation—of the family obstacles which judgment had always opposed to inclination, were dwelt on with a warmth which seemed due to the consequence he was wounding, but was very unlikely to recommend his suit (189).

When Darcy proposes a second time he takes a different tack because he is a different Darcy:

> "The recollection of what I then said, of my conduct, my manners, my expressions during the whole of it, is now, and has been many months, inexpressibly painful to me. Your reproof, so well applied, I shall never forget: 'had you behaved in a more gentleman-like manner.' Those were your words. You know not, you can scarcely conceive, how they have tortured me;—though it was some time, I confess, before I was reasonable enough to allow their justice" (367–368).

Darcy is capable of sympathizing with Elizabeth's rejection of his proposal and of her rejection of Lady Catherine's interference in her personal affairs because he himself was once what his aunt still is. Jane Austen again establishes a relation of sympathetic feeling between Darcy and Elizabeth and ironically forces him to realize that the objection he brought against Elizabeth's family at Hunsford applies as forcefully to his own.

The events from Lydia's elopement to Darcy's proposal clearly

show that Jane Austen is still working out her novel in relation
to the four problems introduced by Darcy's first proposal. Elizabeth accused Darcy of separating Bingley and Jane, of being
unjust to Wickham, of acting generally in an ungentlemanly way.
Darcy, in turn, indicted her family's lack of sense and decorum.
Once stated, the problems are gradually solved. Darcy's letter
to Elizabeth exonerates him of his conduct to Jane and Bingley
and toward Wickham. At Pemberley Elizabeth sees Darcy's
change in manners by his cordial reception of herself and the
Gardiners, and his acceptance of her family is hinted at. But
Jane Austen does not let go of her problems with these solutions.
Each of them must not only be solved by reason but also dissolved
in love. Darcy does not merely right the wrongs he was more or
less guilty of, but he rights them to fault. Darcy's love of Elizabeth is dramatically revealed by his settling a sum of money on
Wickham. The problem of Darcy's doing justice to Wickham is
thus reintroduced and irrevocably solved. So, too, his interference in the love of Bingley and Jane is exonerated when he
returns Bingley to Longbourn, and Bingley proposes. Lady
Catherine's visit to Elizabeth makes Darcy feel how relatively
unimportant his objection to the Bennets is, just as Mrs. Bennet's
treatment of Darcy, when he visits Longbourn with Bingley,
reminds Elizabeth of what there was of justice in Darcy's former
objection to her family. At any rate, Darcy's visit shows how
resilient to change are the good manners—the gentlemanly
conduct—Elizabeth met at Pemberley. Darcy clearly comes to an
unimproved Bennet family, but he comes willingly. He comes to
pluck a flower among the thorns quite conscious that he is going
to be pricked. This is all to his credit and shows that he has come
to understand that the slight consequence of Elizabeth's family
in no way diminishes her desirability; therefore, he comes to
Elizabeth as a man to a woman on the basis of reason and affection. Elizabeth's expression of gratitude for his goodness to
Lydia allows Darcy to tell her that "the wish of giving happiness

to you" added "force to other inducements which led me on" (366). This conversation almost immediately turns into Darcy's second proposal, which shows him accepting the Bennets and bringing to a happy solution the last of the problems raised at Hunsford. The second half of *Pride and Prejudice* clearly shows Darcy and Elizabeth, who have already achieved self-knowledge, moving toward marriage on the bases of reason and gratitude, empathy and love.

The rhythm and modulation of the human events that lead Darcy and Elizabeth to the altar suggest that their marriage is an ideal. They achieve that friendship based on confidence and integrity that Johnson extolled in *The Rambler*, no. 18, as the foundation of true love and happy marriage. It is important in this connection to note how little emphasis is put on the marriage and how much on the courtship. Getting married is not just an end, a standing at the altar; rather, it is a going to the altar. The movement toward marriage in *Pride and Prejudice* is a ritual of human development. In this novel those who just want to get to the altar, no matter what, are different from those who get there in a distinctly human way. Therefore, the marriage of Darcy and Elizabeth compares favorably with that of the Bingleys and of the Gardiners; but it contrasts sharply with the Collinses' marriage, the Wickhams' marriage, and the Bennets' marriage. Their carefully developed love shows Darcy and Elizabeth to be truly human and completely ready to make of their marriage the meaningful union it can be within the limits of the society Jane Austen creates in her novel.

Marriage itself has a social extension in Jane Austen's novels that one must always expect to appear. Marriage is never a matter of personal recognition of individual worth only, important and indispensable as that is. One can presume that the "promise of the introduction" of any Jane Austen novel takes in the assimilation of the couple into a larger context. Jane Austen sees man, "not as a solitary being completed in himself, but only as completed in society."[19] Elizabeth by having her marriage accepted by others sees to it that her personal judgment of Darcy effectively replaces the crude judgments of him that temporarily prevail. As soon as Jane and Mr. Bennet understand that Elizabeth loves Darcy and is marrying him because she loves him, not because he is rich, they rejoice in her engagement. Elizabeth's mother, however, knows nothing about love's relation to respect, reason, and affection. Mrs. Bennet is the poor man's Lady Catherine. Marriage is good because every girl needs a husband to support her; it is the custom. Marriage to a rich man, since it implies indescribable wile, shows the greatest respect for custom.

> "Good gracious! Lord bless me! only think! dear me! Mr. Darcy! Who would have thought it! And is it really true? Oh! my sweetest Lizzy! how rich and how great you will be! What pin-money, what jewels, what carriages you will have! Jane's is nothing to it— nothing at all. I am so pleased—so happy. Such a charming man!— so handsome! so tall!—Oh, my dear Lizzy! pray apologise for my having disliked him so much before. I hope he will overlook it. Dear, dear Lizzy. A house in town! Every thing that is charming! Three daughters married! Ten thousand a year! Oh, Lord! What will become of me. I shall go distracted" (378).

One is hard-put to find any one paragraph in all of Jane Austen where so many exclamation marks are used. To Mrs. Bennet, as her speech reveals, Elizabeth's performance of her duty to marry is superior to anything a mother's heart has known. To Mrs. Bennet's thinking, certainly, her daughter has snatched a grace beyond the reach of a mother's art.

At the end of *Pride and Prejudice* it is clear that Mrs. Bennet is as crass and as stupid as she was at the beginning of the novel. Elizabeth has changed considerably, however. The vain and prejudiced girl has grown into the reasonable and loving woman. It is significant that physical movements correlate with her development. Indeed, Mrs. Bennet's stasis and Elizabeth's dynamism give the novel a total esthetic fitness. It is notable that Mrs. Bennet never leaves Hertfordshire, and for the most part stays in Longbourn. All her world is there. Darcy and Elizabeth first meet in Hertfordshire, where Elizabeth's family alienates Darcy's feelings. At Hunsford, Elizabeth and Darcy meet on more neutral ground. Elizabeth is there as a person to be valued for herself and separated from her family. There Darcy and she come face to face with each others' faults and virtues. Elizabeth is next at Pemberley. At Darcy's Derbyshire estate, she sees him in a new perspective, that of his home. There he is a new man and she a new woman. Lastly, she sees Darcy come to Longbourn, her own home, face her family, and ask her hand. From Hertfordshire, to Hunsford, to Pemberley, to Longbourn: the journey has been for Darcy and Elizabeth as much a journey of the spirit as of the body. The roads of the English countryside have been the way of man between meeting and marriage. By having the principal episodes of *Pride and Prejudice* occur at significant places, Jane Austen carefully coordinates physical and social events with spiritual experiences. The art of travel in Jane Austen is the art of putting people in the right place at the right time. Fielding and Smollett give way to Jane Austen, who places her people in parks and parsonages and who creates excitement in her novels through the movement of the mind and the affections. Her *homo viator* is a man on a more spiritual path than the heroes who trod the road in the novels of her dusty and muddy predecessors. Characteristically, then, the total configuration of events in the plot of the novel shows that in *Pride and Prejudice* the journey from Hertfordshire back to Hertfordshire becomes for Darcy and Elizabeth a movement from pride and prejudice to love.

Now what does it mean to read *Pride and Prejudice* in this way? It means, I think, that one comes to recognize that the plot of the novel expresses the values of the novel. *Pride and Prejudice* dramatizes the possibility of an ordered world in which people are frustrated when they cannot see or when they refuse to recognize what is real in the world about them. Conversely, in this ordered world people who see reality and act reasonably in relation to it find fulfillment and happiness.

In *Pride and Prejudice* Elizabeth Bennet makes a mistake that she finally rectifies. She misjudges Darcy because her prejudice against him leads her to misunderstand a series of incidents in which they are both involved. But by refusing to marry Darcy the first time he proposes, she does not irrevocably create a destiny for herself. Rather her destiny is created for her by his letter, by their accidental meeting at Pemberley, by her sister Lydia's elopement, by Lady Catherine's visit, and by Darcy's generosity. The mistake of one day does not press upon Elizabeth for the rest of her life because the world Jane Austen creates is benign to the degree that one is reasonable and virtuous. Therefore, the mistake of one day brings Elizabeth directly in the middle of *Pride and Prejudice* to a realization of her personal faults, to an understanding of her life, and to an awareness of her character in relation to a reasonable norm according to which men are good or bad. By the time the plot of the novel has reached its midpoint, its heroine is realized as a total and integral human being. After this moment of realization Elizabeth has to be patient and suffer not because of herself, but because of others. The consequences of her first rejection of Darcy are temporary and beneficial. The rejection brings both of them to a realization of their true humanity. Just as the realization overpowers Elizabeth's prejudice, it overpowers Darcy's pride. A series of incidents over which Elizabeth has no control reunites them on the bases of understanding, empathy, gratitude, and love. The novel, then, ends not only with the total individual development of each character but also with his total social development, because personal love is satisfied in marriage and harmonized with society. The most divergent elements come to recognize the reasonableness of the marriage and give it their blessing. Darcy and Elizabeth are assumed into their social order and become exemplars of it in their reasonable and loving marriage. Under these circumstances, therefore, if *Pride and Prejudice* develops four problems and solves them—as I submit it does—it could have ended no sooner than it did.

As a novel that presents a society that has reason for its ideal for action, and marriage as its symbol for personal and societal fulfillment, *Pride and Prejudice* has a plot that controls the presentation of these values. It is so constructed that the characters confront situations that force to our attention those human values that are held to be most important. Through a complex series of interwoven incidents Elizabeth and Darcy are shown acting irrationally, coming to an awareness of their defection from reasonable conduct, experiencing events that enable them to empathize with each other, strengthening their friendship, falling in love, and marrying.

> [The] marriage of Elizabeth and Darcy resolves not only their personal differences but the conflicts they have represented, with the result that the novel provides a final pleasure unique in Jane Austen's fiction, a sense of complete fulfillment analogous to that which marks the end of some musical compositions.[20]

If this reading of *Pride and Prejudice* is valid, a radical reassessment of the significance of plot is needed, for the plot emphasizes an ideal pattern of conduct that shows Jane Austen sounding the classic note:

> If the poet can portray something superior to contemporary practice, it is not in the way of anticipating some later, and quite different code of behaviour, but by an insight into what the conduct of his own people at his own time might be, at its best.[21]

Only in relation to such an ideal does irony—so much emphasized in recent criticism—make sense, because irony demands such an ideal: "Unless there is something about which the author is never ironical," writes C. S. Lewis, "there can be no true irony in the work. 'Total irony'—irony about everything—frustrates itself and becomes insipid."[22] Also, only in relation to such an ideal does money find its place in Jane Austen's created world. Therefore the notion that the form of the novel develops through a vocabulary of mercantile metaphor, which Mark Schorer and Dorothy Van Ghent[23] have proposed, needs rethinking. The plot clearly suggests the true value of money by subjugating it to personal dignity and love in the relationship of Darcy and Elizabeth, and its false value by dramatizing its first importance in the lives of Lady Catherine, Mrs. Bennet, and Charlotte Lucas, none of whom is admirable. In short, in *Pride and Prejudice* the incidents and design of the plot expose an ideal of human conduct and fulfillment that Jane Austen treats neither ironically nor cynically. Rather, she disposes the incidents of the plot in such a way that they shape meaning, direct irony, control diction, and present themselves as an esthetic fact. Consequently, Jane Austen makes plot more than an arrangement of incidents in *Pride and Prejudice*: she makes it a mold of values. And from that mold she strikes a novel of classical delicacy and strength.

4

Education and Integrity in *Mansfield Park*

"Many readers, I suspect, like myself, have found *Mansfield Park*
the most difficult of the works, in the sense that it is there
hardest to be sure of the writer's general intention," wrote R. W.
Chapman in 1948.[1] His remark seems more relevant today than
it was then. Interpretations of *Mansfield Park* in the last twenty-
five years have been remarkable for their diversity—but no more
remarkable than for their dealing with a single salient problem.
There is a rigid social-moral boundary in *Mansfield Park* and that
requires the critic to ask whether an individual's life can be
personally meaningful when it moves within it. Marvin Mudrick
says it cannot.[2] Walton Litz says it can if human freedom is
recognized as essentially limited.[3] Lionel Trilling suggests that
limitation calls forth honesty and heroism,[4] and Joseph Duffy
adds that the limited world of *Mansfield Park* is a bulwark against a
dangerous liberalizing corruption.[5] Howard Babb finds personal
integrity at the heart of unselfishness (the limit of self),[6] and
Thomas Edwards sees in the freedom of the Crawfords an
attempt to destroy integrity by selfishness (the limitless self).[7]
Criticism then sets before one this question: Does or does not
Mansfield Park show that a meaningful personal freedom and
integrity are viable within a traditional pattern of morals and
manners? Such a question can best be answered, I think, by one's
viewing the novel as a dramatization of Fanny Price's education.
In that way one can see the kind of person Fanny's education
makes her and can contrast her with those whose educations and
persons are different from hers.

This study of Fanny's education might properly be begun if

we refer to Samuel Richardson, whom Jane Austen herself found a most congenial teacher.[8] A little reflection makes it quickly evident that *Mansfield Park* has a *Pamela*-like plot. A young girl of no pretensions is brought to the home of a wealthy family and after not a few severe trials becomes the bride of an eligible son. Nevertheless, the Jane Austen who admired Fielding certainly could not think of writing a novel on the moral plan of *Pamela*. Richardson's disaster in that area precluded her making a similar mistake. But the novel of his that Jane Austen most admired was *Sir Charles Grandison*.[9] There, it seems, she found much that was not only congenial to her temperament but much that was also suited to a novel that was to be rigidly devoted to principle and that was to be somewhat less light and bright and sparkling than its immediate predecessor.

In *Sir Charles Grandison* Richardson presents a beleaguered heroine, who is frequently found "perfect" and not infrequently an "angel." Her suitors are so numerous that two thousand pages can, with unhurried decency, scarcely contain them. Pursued by Mr. Greville, dogged by Mr. Fenwick, kidnapped by Sir Hargrave Pollexfen, Harriet Byron will marry no one of them: "Fortune without merit will never do with me, were the man a prince" (IX. 24).[10] Patiently attended in the country by the mild Mr. Orme and waited on in town by the admirable nephew of the lovable Sir Rowland Meredith, she can give her hand to neither, for both fail "to engage her affections." With twelve thousand pounds a year and a mother of amiable disposition and understanding heart, the son of the Countess Dowager of D — can be no more than a brother to Miss Byron. Now Harriet's guardians can find only cause for wonder in all these rejections. Her grandmother Shirley writes with some urgency: "Because you cannot have the man you prefer, [do not] resolve against having any other. Have I not taught you, that marriage is a duty, wherever it can be entered into with prudence?" (IX. 366). But Harriet's principles are as clear as her grandmother's.

Sir Hargrave, Mr. Greville, and Mr. Fenwick are unacceptable because they are not men of moral integrity. As Sir Charles observes, they see in Harriet very little of her true worth:

> "I am afraid that few see in that admirable young lady what I see in her: a mind great and noble: a sincerity beyond that of women: a goodness unaffected, and which shows itself in action, and not merely in words, and outward appearance: a wit lively and inoffensive: and an understanding solid and useful: all which render her a fit companion, either in the social or contemplative hour: and yet she thinks herself not above the knowledge of those duties, the performance of which makes an essential of the female character" (X. 90).

Men like Pollexfen, Greville, and Fenwick have more an eye to Harriet's appearance than to the virtues that Sir Charles lists. Moreover, their conduct has been such that they could not make her happy, as Harriet herself says:

> "A man of free principles, shown by practices as free, can hardly make a tender husband, were a woman able to get over considerations that she ought *not* to get over. Who shall trust for the performance of his *second* duties the man who avoidedly despises his *first*?" (IX. 23)

Mr. Orme and Mr. Fowler—though men "of honour, of virtue, of modesty"—can be esteemed, but not loved. Gratitude is due to the countess dowager's son, but he does not further engage Harriet's affections. It is not to be thought that Miss Byron will give her hand without her heart:

> "I must love the man to whom I would give my hand, well enough to be able, on cool deliberation, to *wish* to be his wife: and for *his* sake (with all my whole heart) choose to quit the single state, in which I am very happy" (IX. 131).

Established then at the very beginning of *Sir Charles Grandison* as a free agent who will not suffer from her guardians what Clarissa did from her parents, Harriet is at liberty to choose her own husband and is assured of her choice being honoured by the Selbys. The man she marries will have to be one who feels as he ought. Also, he must be a man who will make her feel as she ought: "I really think I never shall be in love with anybody, till duty directs inclination" (IX. 76). When Harriet finds the man she can admire and emulate, she will have found the man to whom she can give her heart with her hand.

Sir Charles Grandison, of course, is Harriet's man. He professes and practices the virtue of magnanimity, and everything proves the greatness of his mind and spirit. No problem is too complex for his discrimination, no generosity too prodigal for his pocketbook, no enemy fearsome enough to intimidate or strong enough to overcome him: "a tilting-bout seems no more to him than a game at pushpin" (IX. 320). Sir Charles is so magnanimous that he is frightening:

> "A most *intolerable* superiority!—I wish he would do something wrong; something cruel: if he would but bear malice, would but stiffen his air by resentment, it would be something as a Man, cannot he be lordly and assuming, and where he is so much regarded, I may say *feared*, nod his imperial significance to his vassals about him?—Cannot he be imperious to servants, to show his displeasure with principals? No! it is natural to him to be good and just" (X. 187).

To this Sir Charles, Harriet becomes "a volunteer in her affections" (X. 485). Having found her great man, she has only to remain unalterably attached to him until he can be honorably freed from his impossible engagement with the fair but frenetic Clementina della Parretta. In the end Sir Charles's honor and Harriet's patience are rewarded in marriage. The good man and the good woman become one.

Though more piquant and credibly human, less weighted with moral reflections and less troubled with tear-floods and sigh-tempests, *Mansfield Park* has an affinity with *Sir Charles Grandison* that is almost immediately evident. Mansfield Park may well be an offshoot of Mansfield House, and Sir Thomas Bertram's progenitor may be Sir Thomas Mansfield, "a very good man, and much respected in his neighbourhood," who "was once possessed of a large estate . . ." (X. 405). That "families are little communities; that there are but few solid friendships out of them; and that they help to make up worthily, and to secure the great community, of which they are so many miniatures" (IX. 24) are notions common to *Grandison* and *Mansfield Park*.

Moreover, Fanny Price reminds us of Harriet Byron. Because Fanny's affections are engaged to Edmund Bertram and because Henry Crawford is not a man who feels as he ought, Fanny will not marry him. To give her hand without her heart is an impossibility. No amount of pressure from Sir Thomas, Edmund, Henry, and Mary can force the free choice of Fanny Price. She refuses not to be free within the bounds of duty, and duty does not direct her to sacrifice herself either to the consequence or to the convenience of others. Fanny is scrupulous in trying to let duty direct inclination, in trying to feel as she ought; but only a precise judgment in a moral–emotional situation can define the extent and limit of *ought*.

To feel as one ought is an expression of personal integrity. It presupposes an education in moral principles, an intellectual ability to discriminate obligation in circumstances that relate to those principles, and the possibility of regulating one's feelings according to the dictates of judgment and duty. Personal integrity is intellectual, emotional, and moral. The person who feels as he ought is the good person and the whole person.[11] The responsibility of parents and guardians is to educate their children and charges to such goodness and integrity. The responsibility of those so educated is not to abandon what they have learned. In *Mansfield Park*, Fanny Price is an apt pupil who, in refusing to abandon what she has learned, becomes, in Trilling's phrase, "a Christian heroine." *Mansfield Park* is the story of Fanny's education—of her learning to feel as she ought and of her refusing to feel otherwise.

The plot of *Mansfield Park* develops the meaning of this education by concentrating on Fanny's development as she moves from place to place. Certain places in the novel gradually take on more and more meaning and come to stand in a symbolic relationship to the continuity and integrity of life that are normative in *Mansfield Park*. Jane Austen schools Fanny by changing locales and she schools the reader by asking him to develop an awareness of place as an extension of person. Fanny is brought from her overcrowded and relatively impecunious home in Portsmouth to live at Mansfield Park in the care of her uncle. Sir Thomas's plan is to give Fanny the same advantages of home and education that his daughters enjoy without having her forget "that she is not a *Miss Bertram*."[12] He engages his sister-in-law, Mrs. Norris, to "assist us in our endeavours to choose exactly the right line of conduct" (11).

Mrs. Norris, however, is quite incapable of the nice discriminations Sir Thomas hopes for. She frankly tells Maria and Julia that "it is not at all necessary" that Fanny "should be accomplished as you are;—on the contrary, it is much more desirable that there should be a difference" (19). As a consequence, Fanny is considered by her aunt and her cousins alike "very stupid indeed" and in "a great want of genius and emulation" (19). Because of these and similar attitudes Fanny "was often mortified by their treatment of her"; however, "she thought too lowly of her own claims to feel injured by it" (20). At Mansfield Park Fanny finds herself schooled in humility. She is reared to expect little and is thankful for whatever comes her way.

Through Sir Thomas's kindness Fanny's mind is improved: "Miss Lee taught her French, and heard her read the daily portion of History" (22). More importantly, through her cousin Edmund's generosity she is rejoiced and educated in mind and spirit:

he recommended the books which charmed her leisure hours, he encouraged her taste, and corrected her judgment; he made reading useful by talking to her of what she read, and heightened its attraction by judicious praise. In return for such services she loved him better than anybody in the world except William; her heart was divided between the two (22).

Fanny grows up at Mansfield Park "not unhappily among her cousins" (20), but better prepared than Maria and Julia to endure the departure of Sir Thomas and the arrival of the Crawfords. The sisters are certainly educated and accomplished: "the Miss Bertrams continued to exercise their memories, practice their duets, and grow tall and womanly" (20). "In every thing but disposition, they were admirably taught" (19). The counsels of their Aunt Norris left them "entirely deficient in the less common acquirements of self-knowledge, generosity, and humility" (19). Like Fanny, Maria and Julia have learned a great deal. Unlike Fanny, they have experienced no adversity to temper their vanity; they have had no one to correct their judgment and taste; and they have had no Edmund or William to be worthy objects of their affections. To Fanny, Mansfield Park shapes the limits of a completely meaningful life; to the Bertram sisters it shapes limits only. Consequently, they are morally and emotionally immature when Henry Crawford arrives to flatter them and Sir Thomas leaves and unwittingly allows him to do so.

Henry Crawford's education has taught him that marriage is "Heaven's *last* best gift" (43). Indeed, the "lessons of his uncle," Admiral Crawford, "have quite spoiled him." Henry is, in his sister's words, "the most horrible flirt that can be imagined" (43). Mary, herself, is not unlike her brother in thinking marriage "a manoeuvring business" (46). She too has been in a bad school for matrimony, in Hill Street," the home of Admiral and Mrs. Crawford (46). The meaning of hers and Henry's education and that of the Bertram sisters begins to unfold when the four are thrown together at Sotherton.

The trip to Sotherton is sponsored by Mr. Rushworth, Maria's dull and inept fiancé, who is especially anxious for Henry Crawford's suggestions for the improvement of his property. But little in the line of improvement comes from the visit: "their ramble did not appear to have been . . . at all productive of any thing useful with regard to the object of the day" (104). At Sotherton, the landscape of the soul more than that of the park is found ungainly. There Henry prosecutes his flirtation with the Bertram sisters in the most flagrant manner. Mary displays an irreverence for the clergy and religion that displeases Edmund. And Edmund, himself, neglects Fanny in his attentions to Mary Crawford.

Mrs. Rushworth speaks with more insight than she realizes when she says, "I believe the wilderness will be new to all the party" (90). Henry Crawford later recalls the day as one on which more than a few people were "bewildered" (245). Henry leads Maria and Julia into an emotional wilderness which neither of them is prepared to explore with equanimity. What the narrator says of Julia is true of Maria too:

> the want of that higher species of self-command, that just consideration of others, that knowledge of her own heart, that principle of right which had not formed any essential part of her education, made her miserable . . . (91).

The metaphor of the wilderness is also called into play in the conversation of Mary and Edmund. Mary, who has learned of Edmund's decision to be a clergyman, urges him to change his mind and go into law:

> "Go into the law! with as much ease as I was told to go into this wilderness."
> "Now you are going to say something about law being the worst wilderness of the two, but I forestall you; remember I have forestalled you" (94).

The law is indeed a wilderness for Edmund; whereas the

Church provides through education a path for men who might otherwise be bewildered in life.

> ". . . I cannot call that situation nothing, which has the charge of all that is of the first importance to mankind, individually or collectively considered, temporally or eternally—which has the guardianship of religion and morals, and consequently of the manners which result from their influence.
>
> .   .   .   .
>
> The *manners* I speak of, might rather be called *conduct*, perhaps, the result of good principles; the effect, in short, of those doctrines which it is their duty to teach and recommend; and it will, I believe, be every where found, that as the clergy are, or are not what they ought to be, so are the rest of the nation." (92–93)

The conduct of Crawford and Maria Bertram seems patently in want of some such direction at Sotherton. Crawford has come to change Sotherton, but Sotherton and Maria are one. The estate is not yet altered, nor is Maria yet Mrs. Rushworth; therefore, both occupy Crawford's attention.

> "I do not think that *I* shall ever see Sotherton again with so much pleasure as I do now. Another summer will hardly improve it to me."
>
> After a moment's embarrassment the lady replied, "You are too much a man of the world not to see with the eyes of the world. If other people think Sotherton improved, I have no doubt that you will" (98).

The conversation turns on the same point when Crawford puns on the word "prospects," making it refer to both marriage and landscape.

> "Your prospects . . . are too fair to justify want of spirits. You have a very smiling scene before you"
>
> "Do you mean literally or figuratively? Literally I conclude. Yes, certainly, the sun shines and the park looks very cheerful.

But unluckily that iron gate, that ha-ha, give me a feeling of restraint and hardship. I cannot get out, as the starling said.'' As she spoke, and it was with expression, she walked to the gate: he followed her. ''Mr. Rushworth is so long fetching this key!''

''And for the world you would not get out without the key and without Mr. Rushworth's authority and protection, or I think you might with little difficulty pass round the edge of the gate, here, with my assistance; I think it might be done, if you really wished to be more at large, and could allow yourself to think it not prohibited.''

''Prohibited! nonsense! I certainly can get out that way, and I will'' (99).

The young man and the young lady flirting, as well as the references to the sun and the iron gates, suggest the classic lines about another set of lovers making similar use of another day:

> Let us roll all our strength and all
> Our sweetness up into one ball,
> And tear our pleasures with rough strife
> Through the iron gates of life:
> Thus, though we cannot make our sun
> Stand still, yet we will make him run.[13]

And if ''Time's winged chariot'' is not hurrying near, Mr. Rushworth is. So Henry and Maria slip past the iron gates and out of sight.

Education is meaningless if the person educated is unable to act freely and responsibly when alone. With Sir Thomas away, the Bertram sisters, like Fanny, are alone. Unlike Fanny, they value only their freedom, not its responsibilities. Indeed, they have not been educated to responsibility, but to vanity: ''principle, active principle, had been wanting, . . . they had never been properly taught to govern their inclinations and tempers, by that sense of duty which can alone suffice'' (463). Also, neither has known either the meaning or the expression of true affection.

The relation between love and esteem has never occurred to them. Henry Crawford is the first man to attract Julia, but he is hardly a worthy man. Maria is engaged to Rushworth more because of ambition than admiration. Both sisters are prime targets for Henry Crawford, whom Admiral Croft has taught that the game of love is satisfying only as long as it is played at: marriage is "heaven's *last* best gift." Maria and Julia have neither the moral nor the emotional maturity to cope with a seasoned hunter like Henry Crawford.

Edmund shows greater steadiness of character and purpose than his sisters, but his good judgment begins to fail under the influence of Mary Crawford's attractions. His resolution to be ordained is held to, but Mary's want of religious principles is overlooked. Mary also so occupies Edmund's attention that he leaves Fanny alone in the wilderness for an hour, having promised to stay away only a few minutes.

What characterizes the events at Sotherton, then, is the threat of change. One's personal integrity and the integrity of his relationships are endangered. To the degree one's integrity is seriously endangered something is wanting. Sotherton announces that in *Mansfield Park* the notion that "by their fruits you will know them" is a reality, not just an idea. The fruit of a total education is integrity; of bad breeding, its loss.

Interestingly enough, in this connection, Edmund warns Rushworth against any improvements but his own at Sotherton:

> ". . . Had I a place to new fashion, I should never put myself into the hands of an improver. I would rather have an inferior degree of beauty, of my own choice, and acquired progressively. I would rather abide by my own blunders than by his" (56).

Edmund is in effect urging Rushworth to preserve the integrity of his relation to his own property. Rushworth, however, is deaf to this advice and calls Henry Crawford to his estate.

The threat to the integrity of Rushworth's relation to his

estate is an emblem of threats to integrity on the human level.
Edmund's ordination is attacked and the fulfillment of Fanny's
love for him is endangered by Mary Crawford. Her brother
successfully destroys the sisterly regard of Julia and Maria for
each other by calculatingly turning it to jealousy. More seriously,
he tampers with the integrity of Maria's engagement to Mr.
Rushworth. The attacks that Henry and Mary make on personal
integrity and the integrity of relationships at Mansfield Park
reveal their lack of breeding in an inability to value what they
ought. Sotherton shows Maria and Julia—and Edmund too—
abrogating their duty to feel as they ought and to act accordingly.
The excursion to Sotherton puts to the test the total education of
all who visit there, and not a few are found wanting. Fanny
Price, sitting on a bench and watching those who pass by, sees
and judges all these events. She gets an unfiltered view of human
relationships when at Sotherton her schoolroom becomes the
wilderness and her text the aberrations of the heart.[14]

Of Tom Bertram's production of *Lovers' Vows* Lionel Trilling
has argued that if we are aware of the nineteenth-century
concern with "the hygiene of the self, . . . we are prepared to
take seriously an incident in *Mansfield Park* that on its face is
perfectly absurd." One can only applaud the relation Trilling
makes between this concern and Plato's fear that "the impersona-
tion of any other self will diminish the integrity of the real self."[15]
One can nevertheless only regret the attempt to see the episode as
otherwise absurd. Certainly the production of the play makes the
already existing threats to integrity more acute at the same time
that it introduces new ones. Trilling argues that "it is never made
clear why it is so very wrong for young people in a dull country
house to put on a play,"[16] but this is simply not so. To put on the
play, Edmund argues,

> "would show great want of feeling on my father's account, absent
> as he is, and in some degree of constant danger; and it would be

imprudent, I think, with regard to Maria, whose situation is a very delicate one, considering every thing, extremely delicate" (125).

Not only is the integrity of the Rushworth-Bertram engagement seriously endangered by the intimacy the play demands, but the integrity of the father-son relationship is threatened as well. "I am convinced that my father will totally disapprove it," says Edmund (126). Clearly, as far as his younger brother is concerned, Tom's inclination to stage a play is a violation of his duty to Sir Thomas; it is a unique example of the son failing to feel as he ought toward his father.

Edmund objects to the proposal for a theater too. He objects to the alterations a theater will demand as strongly as he objected to the improvement of Mr. Rushworth's estate by hands other than the owner's. Tom Bertram as theater manager is as much an interloper at Mansfield Park as Henry Crawford as landscape artist was at Sotherton. "I think a theatre ought not to be attempted," argues Edmund. "It would be taking liberties with my father's house in his absence which could not be justified" (127). But Tom's delicacy toward such a consideration is already on record: "My father's room will be an excellent green-room. It seems to join the billiard-room on purpose" (125). The scheme of acting the play is a bad one, then, not only because it threatens the integrity of the self, as Trilling has wisely observed, but also because it threatens the son's relationship to his father and the father's relationship to his house. The play endangers meaningful and traditional symbols of order.[17]

Nevertheless, in spite of "the disadvantages of decorum and education" that must be struggled through, the Bertram sisters are eager for the play—though Julia's ardor abates when Maria is chosen to play Agatha opposite Crawford's Frederick. Even Edmund, after arguing against the play, is drawn into it by his concern for Mary Crawford. The reasoning by which Edmund justifies the step demonstrates to Fanny the strength of his attachment to Mary and the dangers to his judgment and independence that attend on it. Inevitably, the play allows Mary to tamper further with Edmund's plan for ordination, and it allows Henry to disturb further Maria's relation to her fiancé and her sister. Also, for the first time, the play threatens Fanny's role as spectator and judge of the game of life. It involves her in the reality of the moment and gives her the opportunity to prove that her determination is equal to her discretion. To act a part in a play that Sir Thomas must certainly disapprove of, Fanny judges, is to be less than dutiful to her uncle. Therefore, no amount of pressure can overcome her resolution not to act. Fanny proves her integrity and shows that between a good education and a good action there is a continuity that can and should be maintained.

Sotherton and the play at the Park show the value of Fanny's rounded education. When Sir Thomas returns, the play is prevented and the theater dismantled. Fanny, like Edmund, has judged correctly the obligations of all to the master of Mansfield Park. Fanny has also shown herself emotionally stable. Neither her love for Edmund nor her feeling of duty toward Sir Thomas waver with the shock of romance that Henry Crawford brings to the Park. Fanny has also shown a steadfastness against pressure directed against what she judges and feels to be right. Sotherton and the play advance Fanny's education too. She meets her first rake in Henry Crawford and learns well the lesson he teaches her. She learns, as Harriet Byron had said, that a "man of free principles, shown by practices as free, can hardly make a tender husband, were a woman able to get over considerations that she ought *not* to get over." Maria Bertram at the altar with Mr. Rushworth proves the faithlessness of Henry Crawford as her lover. The lesson Fanny learns is very important because on it will come to depend her self-integrity and the continuity of her love for Edmund and her duty toward his father.

The return of Sir Thomas, as I have said, shows that Fanny has

been letter-perfect in her judgments on events at Mansfield Park.
His return removes almost immediately two of the threats that
had been developing. Edmund is ordained and Maria married.
Julia accompanies Maria on her wedding journey as an anodyne
to Mr. Rushworth, and Edmund is now very busy at Thornton
Lacey. Frequently alone at the Park, Fanny becomes the center
of Sir Thomas' attentions, and of Henry Crawford's too. Consequently, Fanny becomes the one threatened.

When the Bertram sisters leave Mansfield Park, there is only
one girl left in the field. Henry Crawford refuses to give up the
chase with so interesting a prey afoot.

> "And how do you think I mean to amuse myself, Mary, on the days
> that I do not hunt? I am grown too old to go out more than three
> times a week; but I have a plan for the intermediate days, and what
> do you think it is?"
>
> "To walk and ride with me, to be sure."
>
> "Not exactly, though I shall be happy to do both, but *that* would
> be exercise only to my body, and I must take care of my mind.
> Besides *that* would be all recreation and indulgence, without the
> wholesome alloy of labour, and I do not like to eat the bread of
> idleness. No, my plan is to make Fanny Price in love with me."
>
> "Fanny Price! Nonsense! No, no. You ought to be satisfied with
> her two cousins."
>
> "But I cannot be satisfied without Fanny Price, without making
> a small hole in Fanny Price's heart" (229).

But taking aim at an elusive prey requires a good eye, so Henry
begins to notice things: Fanny is quiet and modest (229); "her
air, her manner, her tout ensemble" are attractive (230); above
all, she is a challenge: "her looks say, 'I will not like you, I am
determined not to like you,' and I say, she shall" (230). When
William Price arrives, Fanny becomes captivating. The hart
indeed catches the hunter:

> "Fanny's   attractions   increased—increased   two-fold—for   the

sensibility which beautified her complexion and illumined her countenance, was an attraction in itself. He was no longer in doubt of the capabilities of her heart. She had feeling, genuine feeling. It would be something to be loved by such a girl, to excite the first ardour of her young, unsophisticated mind! She interested him more than he had foreseen" (235–236).

Only Fanny's acceptance of a necklace surreptitiously given and two dances at the ball Sir Thomas plans in her honor are further needed to bring Henry to his knees. He announces his capitulation to his sister, "You must be aware that I am quite determined to marry Fanny Price" (291).

It requires only Fanny's refusal to amaze not only Henry and Mary, but Sir Thomas and Edmund as well. The reader, however, is ready to receive it, for he knows that Fanny has found Crawford's treatment of the Bertram sisters the work of "a corrupted mind" (225). To Fanny, Crawford is man who "can feel nothing as he ought" (227). He is utterly without integrity. To Sir Thomas's plea, she can only answer, "I—I cannot like him, Sir, well enough to marry him" (315). For the first time in her life Fanny refuses to accede to her uncle's wishes, and her refusal places her under the severest strain.

"Here is a young man of sense, of character, of temper, of manners, and of fortune, exceedingly attached to you, and seeking your hand in the most handsome and disinterested way; and let me tell you, Fanny, that you may live eighteen years longer in the world, without being addressed by a man of half Mr. Crawford's estate, or a tenth part of his merits. Gladly would I have bestowed either of my own daughters on him. Maria is nobly married—but had Mr. Crawford sought Julia's hand, I should have given it to him with superior and more heartfelt satisfaction than I gave Maria's to Mr. Rushworth." After half a moment's pause—"And I should have been very much surprised had either of my daughters, on receiving a proposal of marriage at any time, which might carry with it only *half* the eligibility of *this*, immediately and peremptorily, and without

paying my opinion or my regard the compliment of any consultation, put a decided negative on it. I should have been much
surprised, and much hurt, by such a proceeding. I should have
thought it a gross violation of duty and respect. *You* are not to be
judged by the same rule. You do not owe me the duty of a child.
But, Fanny, if your heart can acquit you of *ingratitu de*—''

He ceased. Fanny was by this time crying so bitterly, that angry
as he was, he would not press that article farther. Her heart was
almost broke by such a picture of what she appeared to him; by
such accusations, so heavy, so multiplied, so rising in dreadful
gradation! Self-willed, obstinate, selfish, and ungrateful. He thought
her all this. She had deceived his expectations; she had lost his
good opinion. What was to become of her? (319)

Fanny's grief is exacerbated by Crawford's unfeeling persistence,
his sister's urging, and Edmund's interest in Mary. Fanny's
situation is now the same in relation to her uncle's wishing her to
marry as it was earlier in relation to Tom Bertram's desire that
she play a role:

> "You must excuse me, indeed you must excuse me," cried
> Fanny. . . . Her entreaty had no effect on Tom; he only said again
> what he said before; and it was not merely Tom, for the requisition
> was now backed by Maria and Mr. Crawford, and Mr. Yates, with
> an urgency which differed from his, but in being more gentle or
> more ceremonious, and which altogether was quite overpowering
> to Fanny . . . (146).

The sad difference is that now Edmund is not willing to say,
"Her judgment may be quite . . . safely trusted.—Do not urge
her any more" (147). Edmund's involvement with Mary Crawford confuses him in a way that Mary herself cannot be confused
about Fanny: "From my soul I do not think she would marry . . .
without love; that is, if there is a girl in the world capable of being
uninfluenced by ambition, I can suppose it her . . ." (293).
Mary understands that, like Harriet Byron, Fanny Price will not
give her hand without her heart.

At this point in *Mansfield Park* Fanny's resolution is tried to the utmost. Indeed, Sir Thomas's speech to Fanny recalls Mr. Harlow's ordering Clarissa to marry the detestable Mr. Soames. The many raucous voices that supported his in *Clarissa* have their modulated counterparts here in those of Crawford, Mary, and Edmund. At this point in *Mansfield Park*, more than at any other, we see that Jane Austen has gone to school to Richardson, the master of moral pressure, in an effort to dramatize the relation of education to the resilience of the Christian heroine. Fanny holds out against pressure, just as Harriet Byron and Clarissa Harlow did, because her freedom and integrity demand it. Fanny, in her enlightened obstinancy, supports the meaning of life that she has been educated to respect. Sir Thomas' position as a counterforce is therefore richly ironic.

In fact, the moments that Sir Thomas spends with Fanny may be considered the most ironic ones in the novel if for no other reason than that they take place in the East room, an "apartment . . . spacious and . . . meet for walking about in, and thinking, and of which she had now for sometime been . . . mistress" (150). Sir Thomas bears down heavily on Fanny's freedom in the single room of the house that is a symbol of her freedom:

> gradually, as her value for the comforts of it increased, she had added to her possessions, and spent more of her time there; and having nothing to oppose her, had so naturally and so artlessly worked herself into it, that it was now generally admitted to be her's. The East room as it had been called, ever since Maria Bertram was sixteen, was now considered Fanny's, almost as decidedly as the white attic [her bedroom] . . . (151).

Furthermore, the East room had been Fanny's school room, "so-called till the Miss Bertrams would not allow it be called so any longer" (150). Thus the place of Fanny's schooling is seen to be both the seat and analogue of her freedom. The integral relation of her education to her judgment is mirrored in the school and East room's being one.[18]

Fanny has been educated to exercise her freedom by judging for herself. In the East room she had decided a second time not to act in *Lovers' Vows* were she asked again. In the East room she disagreed with Edmund's decision to act the part of Anhalt. In the East room, in short, she has judged her duty to Sir Thomas correctly and has had as thanks "the charge of obstinancy and ingratitude" from his children (150). Now Sir Thomas himself comes to the East room and tells Fanny:

> "You have shewn me that you can be wilful and perverse, that you can and will decide for yourself, without any consideration or deference for those who have surely some right to guide you— without even asking their advice" (318).

Fanny cannot answer Sir Thomas because her "ill opinion" of Henry Crawford "was founded chiefly on observations, which, for her cousins' sake, she could scarcely dare mention to their father" (317). Fanny sat on the bench of desolation at Sotherton and had a seat in the theater at Mansfield: she went to school in the wilderness and in the billiard room and got an education that Sir Thomas then in Antigua did not dream of and that she cannot now tell him of. In ignorance, then, he puts himself in the awkward position of asking Fanny to repudiate the meaning of an education she could not have got were she not his ward. This sure and certain contradiction can only make wonderful the opinion of those who find in *Mansfield Park* Jane Austen's retreat from irony.

Exile is the last form of pressure that Sir Thomas, with a certain lack of finesse, imposes on Fanny:

> It was a medicinal project upon his niece's understanding, which he must consider as at present diseased. A residence of eight or nine years in the abode of wealth and plenty had a little disordered her powers of comparing and judging. Her Father's house would, in all probability, teach her the value of a good income; and he trusted that she would be the wiser and happier woman, all her life, for the experiment he had devised (369).

Quite explicitly, Sir Thomas sends Fanny to Portsmouth for the last bit of her education before she leaves his house as a bride. The tawdriness of Portsmouth is to make Everingham, Crawford's estate, more immediately appealing. Sir Thomas is partially right and partially wrong. Fanny has identified her life so completely with Mansfield Park—intellectually and emotionally, morally and physically—that only it, not Everingham, is missed.

> The elegance, propriety, regularity, harmony—and perhaps, above all, the peace and tranquillity of Mansfield, were brought to her remembrance every hour of the day, by the prevalence of every thing opposite to them *here* (391).

So Fanny does learn a lesson in value, but not exactly the one Sir Thomas had hoped for.

Beyond this, Fanny develops in other ways too. Portsmouth strengthens her independence, which was reaching toward maturity at Mansfield Park. Fanny is not only called upon to judge and to act, but to do so without recourse to Edmund. In a most salutary manner, she takes her sister Susan in hand:

> She gave advice; advice too sound to be resisted by a good understanding, and given so mildly and considerately as not to irritate an imperfect temper; and she had the happiness of observing its good effects not unfrequently; more was not expected by one, who, while seeing all the obligation and expediency of submission and forbearance, saw also with sympathetic acuteness of feeling, all that must be hourly grating to a girl like Susan (397).

The good effects of Fanny's education are propagated by her independent action in Portsmouth. But like the wilderness and the theater, Portsmouth is not a pleasant seat of learning. So at precisely the moment that Fanny is beginning to feel the length of her stay, she is recalled to Mansfield Park. The Bertram sisters have proved the inadequacy of their education—Maria by adultery, Julia by eloping—and Fanny is needed. She returns home to find a father brooding over the education of his daughters:

> He feared that principle, active principle, had been wanting, that
> they had never been properly taught to govern their inclinations
> and tempers, by that sense of duty which can alone suffice. They
> had been instructed theoretically in their religion, but never
> required to bring it into daily practice. . . . He had meant them
> to be good, but his cares had been directed to the understanding
> and manners, not the disposition; and of the necessity of self-
> denial and humility, he feared they had never heard from any
> lips that could profit them (463).

When Sir Thomas deplores his daughters' failure "to govern
their inclinations and tempers" by a "sense of duty," he is
really scoring their refusal to feel as they ought. And when he
deplores their being directed in "understanding and manners"
alone, he is really saying that his daughters have not been educated morally and emotionally as well as intellectually and socially.

The novel almost becomes deterministic at this point because
Sir Thomas suggests such a degree of continuity between character, action, and education that to deny one a well rounded education seems to be to deny him the ability to act with integrity.
While Sir Thomas' statement is interesting in this light, it seems
a little too rigorous for the drama of *Mansfield Park*.[19] Maria and
Julia are blameworthy, as are the Crawfords, because they could
have improved themselves but did not and because the moral
principles upheld by society were clearly in opposition to their
actions. Sir Thomas blames himself because he realizes that had
he done a little more a little earlier he would have made life at
its difficult moments a little easier for his daughters. And Sir
Thomas sees his mistakes more clearly because the Prices have
educated him: in Susan's

> usefulness, in Fanny's excellence, in William's continued good
> conduct, and rising fame, and in the general well-doing and success
> of the other members of the family, all assisting to advance each
> other, and doing credit to his countenance and aid, Sir Thomas
> saw repeated, and for ever repeated reason to rejoice in what he

had done for them all, and acknowledge the advantages of early hardship and discipline, and the consciousness of being born to struggle and endure (473).

If nothing else, *Mansfield Park* shows itself—even with its rapid, undramatized ending—a novel that supports a moral continuity that is grounded in the education of the intellect and feelings as well as the will. In this continuity *Mansfield Park* is inflexible and almost parabolic. In fact, it reminds one of Hogarth's "pictur'd Morals"[20] in its relentlessness. Its subject is not marriage made à la mode or a rake's progress to Bedlam through moral regression. Rather its subject is the education of a human being as a total person and its emphasis the need for instruction that is moral and emotional as well as intellectual and social. Those who indulge their feelings haphazardly and their wit and grace gallantly are invariably those without moral principle and those whom life wears thin with a little abrasiveness. They do not feel as they ought; duty does not direct affection for them; they have not, in Johnson's phrase, "taught their passions to move at the command of virtue."[21] Therefore they inevitably suffer the fate of the morally weak who are strongly passionate. As in Hogarth, so in Jane Austen: a single principle illuminates a series of pictures of life that are themselves complex. The Sotherton excursion and the play at the Park; the East room; Portsmouth and Mansfield Park evoke as much of life's variety and difficulty as the places in which Tom Rakewell finds himself and his company. But in Jane Austen's novel the central figure is not a rake and the central issue is not the threat that comes to all moral and human values through the power of money.[22] Rather the central issue is the threat to the integrity of the self that comes from an easy life lived without principle. *Mansfield Park* tells us that the only meaningful human freedom is found in a self-integrity that is measured by the constant of principle; therefore, to be truly oneself is to feel as one ought. As Trilling has said, "It discovers in principle the path to the wholeness of self which is peace."[23]

That is why the novel emphasizes integrity found in a continuity proper to one's state in life as it comes (somewhat too rapidly) to a close. Sir Thomas as parent and guide learns the meaning of education and fatherhood. Edmund as a clergyman regains the judgment that his dangerous connection with Mary had so frequently muddled. Julia is reconciled with her father, humbling herself and "wishing to be forgiven" (462). And Fanny is elevated by love from niece to daughter and from cousin to wife. Not long thereafter, she and Edmund move from Thornton Lacey to the parsonage at the Park:

> . . . The acquisition of Mansfield living by the death of Dr. Grant, occurred just after they had been married long enough to begin to want an increase of income, and feel their distance from the paternal abode an inconvenience.
>
> On that event they removed to Mansfield, and the parsonage there, which under each of its two former owners, Fanny had never been able to approach but with some painful sensation of restraint or alarm, soon grew as dear to her heart, and as thoroughly perfect in her eyes, as every thing else, within the view and patronage of Mansfield Park, had long been (473).

Jane Austen establishes the final symbolic relation between place and value and brings her novel to a close. Her husband brings Fanny to a "house / Where all's accustomed, ceremonious." For how, the novel seems finally to ask, "but in custom and in ceremony / Are innocence and beauty born?"[24]

5

Action and Symbol in *Emma*

Emma is a deceptive novel; so deceptive, in fact, that more than one critic has characterized it as "a novel without a plot."[1] It is true that *Emma* reminds one in some ways of a novel by Henry James, who found plots nefarious,[2] because Emma, like Isabel Archer, seems to be a young woman affronting her destiny[3] and, like other Jamesian heroines, seems to function as a central intelligence. But Wayne Booth has adequately demonstrated the difference between the reader's seeing with an Austen heroine and seeing with a Jamesian one. "Unlike the central intelligences of James and his successors," he writes, " 'Jane Austen' has learned nothing at the end of the novel that she did not know at the beginning. She needed to learn nothing. She knew everything of importance already."[4] This observation is indispensable to an understanding of how Emma affronts her destiny in Jane Austen's novel. The heroine's destiny is no mystery to the author because she knows the limits of the world in which Emma takes life. Jane Austen creates the plot that delimits perfectly Emma's world and Emma's destiny. The plot develops by allowing Emma to try to push beyond the prescribed limits and by having Mr. Knightley remind her again and again that she cannot do so. The novel unfolds with Emma's making great efforts to shape an unreal destiny in an unreal world and with Mr. Knightley predicting to her a real destiny in the real world. He simply tells Emma how reality will shape her when she insists that she is going to shape it. The thrust against reality and the counter-thrust of reality establish a rhythm of action in *Emma* and give the plot a predictable structure.

Within this structure Jane Austen uses the realities of her delimited world in a symbolic way, first to challenge Emma's ingenuity and then to test her honesty. They eventually assert their ineluctable existence in her consciousness, much to the embarrassment of her conscience. But Emma accepts these realities just as she accepts Mr. Knightley's judgments; her marriage, in fact, comes to stand as a symbolic realization of her finding meaning in a delimited world and of her understanding the meaning of its symbols. "Marriage to an intelligent, amiable, good, and attractive man is the best thing that can happen to this heroine," asserts Wayne Booth, who continues with some acerbity, "the readers who do not experience it as such are, I am convinced, far from knowing what Jane Austen is about— whatever they may say about the 'bitter spinster's' attitude toward marriage."[5]

If one sees *Emma* as Booth does, one will have to judge the novel's final event as a meaningful culmination of its action. The marriage of Emma Woodhouse to George Knightley must be seen as just the right ending, and the statement of the narrator, who understands Emma's delimited world perfectly, has to be accepted rather literally: "the wishes, the hopes, the confidence, the predictions of the small band of true friends who witnessed the ceremony, were fully answered in the perfect happiness of the union."[6] Emma has come to see reality for what it is, and suitably she marries the man who best represents what is true and what is good in that reality. But, of course, critics do not unanimously agree with this reading of *Emma* and of its conclusion. "Oh, Miss Austen, it was *not* a good solution; it was a bad solution, an unhappy ending, could we see beyond the last pages of the book," writes G. B. Stern,[7] who does not want for sympathetic company.[8]

Marvin Mudrick, for instance, indicated that "*Emma* can be read as the story of a spoiled rich girl who is corrected by defeat and love, and who lives happily ever after."[9] But he soon found this brief but felicitous statement too unhappily simple and shortly concluded "that there is no happy ending, no easy equilibrium, if we care to project confirmed exploiters like Emma and Frank Churchill into the future of their marriages."[10] Emma and Mr. Knightley do not live "happily ever after" because she is never really "corrected." Jane Austen's novel, according to Mudrick, has about it none of the "moral finickiness" of *Mansfield Park*[11] and consequently we cannot expect to find any moral reformation in the heroine. Moreover, "the story tells itself, and nothing seems more superfluous than inquiry or deep thought about it."[12] But certainly the critic's own twenty-six page essay gives the lie to this assertion. "This is not an easy book to read," writes Reginald Farrer.[13] And Lionel Trilling insists that "*Emma* is more difficult than any of the hard books we admire."[14] *Emma* is precisely the kind of novel that invites thought, and rumination suggests that in its own way the novel is as deeply involved with a personal and humane morality as any other of Jane Austen's works,[15] that the character of Emma is profoundly changed in the course of the story, and that there is more reason to uphold the validity of a happy ending than to suspect it. An examination of the principal action of the novel and some of the more preeminent symbols that give that action definition should make this clear: Emma is salutarily defeated in her attempts to dominate Harriet Smith and Jane Fairfax, is worried into a revaluation of her proper function in life by confrontation with Mrs. Elton, and is rescued from her domineering egoism by Mr. Knightley's sense of reality and by his love.[16]

Jane Austen's novel begins on the day that Emma's governess and companion becomes Mr. Weston's wife. It begins with the problem that confronts Emma, who is left at Hartfield, when Miss Taylor moves to Randalls. Anne Taylor

> had been a friend and companion such as few possessed, intelligent, well-informed, useful, gentle, knowing all the ways of the family, interested in all its concerns, and peculiarly interested in herself, in

every pleasure, every scheme of her's;—one to whom she could speak every thought as it arose, and who had such an affection for her as could never find fault (6).

With her friend's disappearance Emma wonders how she will be able "to bear the change" (6). How will Emma Woodhouse, who is used to "having rather too much her own way" (5), have any power at all without anyone to direct? How will Emma Woodhouse, who is used to thinking "a little too well of herself" (5), get along without anyone to admire her? How will Emma Woodhouse "bear the change?" This is the problem that Jane Austen begins with and continues to develop till she concludes the novel by replacing Miss Taylor with Mr. Knightley.

Suitably, Mr. Knightley steps into Hartfield the day Miss Taylor steps out. Proleptically, the novel begins by suggesting its ending. We are introduced at the beginning of *Emma* to the same picturesque group[17] with which it ends: Mr. Knightley, Emma, and Mr. Woodhouse together at Hartfield. The action of the novel takes us through a series of incidents that teach Emma the meaning of what Mr. Knightley calls "true gentility" (65) and that make it possible for him to return to Hartfield as Emma's husband in the last chapter of the novel. The structure of *Emma* brings the novel full circle, for it begins and ends with a wedding and it begins and ends with Mr. Knightley, Emma, and Mr. Woodhouse at Hartfield.

The little group itself is significant in each case. It suggests dramatically that there will be no wedding at the end of *Emma* unless the relationship among the persons who form the group changes in the course of the action. Emma is dramatically placed between her father and Mr. Knightley. At the beginning of the novel and during the course of much of it Emma is more like her father than her future husband. Emma must be weaned from that relationship and establish a new one before she can marry Mr. Knightley. She must be weaned from a false superiority and selfishness—from a spurious kind of gentility—and come to accept reality and human relations in the way that Mr. Knightley does before she can become his wife.

Mr. Woodhouse is one of Jane Austen's superb comic creations. Certainly she is indebted to Laurence Sterne for him, for Mr. Woodhouse is the Uncle Topy of the surgery and medicine bottle, if not the battlefield and cannon ball. Mr. Woodhouse is a man who deplores inconvenience of any kind. He avoids it by becoming a hypochondriac and by relating all the world to himself, rather than the other way round. He sees all that is normal in relation to his abnormality and sets up a convenient standard of judgment for dealing with the world. Mrs. Weston is "poor Miss Taylor" because her marriage inconveniences his household. Wedding cake and roast pork are not to be eaten by others because they upset his stomach. He cannot understand why a "basin of gruel," which he favors, is not "taken every evening by every body" (100–101). People should not speak too rapidly because rapid speech "rather hurts the ear" of Mr. Woodhouse (279). Young folk should not dance because they are likely to sweat, and sweating gives him a chill. "The sea is very rarely of use to anybody," says Mr. Woodhouse, because "I am sure it almost killed me once" (101). Emma's picture of Harriet is at fault because it depicts its subject out of doors "with only a little shawl over her shoulders" (48). Jane Fairfax must certainly change her stockings after walking in the rain or suffer the con- consequences of a cold: "Young ladies are delicate plants. They should take care of their health and their complexion" (294). No coachman is safe save James because he has never given Mr. Woodhouse a fright or a spill. It is even necessary, Mr. Wood- house tells his daughter, "to spare our horses when we can" (252).

Mr. Woodhouse is a continual source of laughter in *Emma*, but he is more than that. He is an example of a radical detachment from reality. (His every speech shows him to be the novel's great centrifugal character who spins out a world of his own just as Miss Bates's show her to be its antithetical centripetal one who reels in every stray scrap of Highbury news.) Mr. Woodhouse reduces his relations to others and to the world to a simple system: he wants neither to inconvenience nor to be inconvenienced, he wants neither to pain nor to be pained. Consequently he is at once the most gentle and egocentric character in *Emma*. His daughter is in no immediate danger of absorbing her father's gentleness, but he represents the danger of detachment from reality by way of egoism that she is liable to. Certainly Mr. Woodhouse has everything his way. Indeed, he is the only character in the novel who continuously has Emma under his control. She even refuses to marry Mr. Knightley if it means leaving her father, and Mr. Woodhouse does not consent to the marriage until fear of poachers makes a man in the house necessary to his peace of mind. Mr. Woodhouse's system, subconscious and genteely neurotic to be sure, is flawless. It makes him everyone's friend and everyone's object of compassion. His weakness is his strength.

Mr. Woodhouse represents an extreme toward which Emma is prone. Emma likes having everything her own way. She is introduced into the novel as a young woman who has had "little to distress or vex her" (5). At twenty-one she is used to self-reliance, "the shadow of authority being now long passed away."

> The real evils indeed of Emma's situation were the power of having rather too much her own way, and a disposition to think a little too well of herself; these were the disadvantages which threatened alloy to her many enjoyments (5).

Emma Woodhouse, "handsome, clever, and rich" (5), likes very much to dominate and to be superior, and as the first lady of Highbury society she enjoys prerogatives that flatter her disposition. As mistress of Hartfield and Highbury Emma is in danger of subjugating the world to herself and of living an illusion. Her health and beauty, power and determination place her in the danger of following vigorously in the footsteps of her faltering father.

Mr. Knightley is Emma's only hope. For he stands with reality. Unlike the retired and secluded Mr. Woodhouse, Mr. Knightley is gregarious. We find him at Hartfield, at Randalls, at Donwell Abbey; with the Bateses, with the Martins, with the Coxes; on horseback, on foot, in a carriage; at a dance, at a dinner, at a tea. He is not a retired valetudinarian; he is a gentleman with farms to run and a magistrate with affairs to see to. His farms keep him close to the earth; his magistracy calls on his judgment and connects him with a cross-section of humanity. Both callings force him to a closeness with life. Mr. Knightley is the most prominent gentleman in Highbury society as well as the master of Donwell Abbey. But he does not relish his superiority in the same way that Emma does hers. Mr. Knightley is not interested in dominating, as Emma is. While not disregarding social rank and prestige, he regards intrinsic human worth as more important. He is continuously more interested in the person than the position. To him Jane Fairfax is a better person than Frank Churchill, even though he saves her by marriage. To him Miss Bates is worthy of an apology from Emma. To him Mrs. Elton is inferior to the illegitimate Harriet. To him Robert Martin, the farmer, is a man of true gentility. It is Mr. Knightley who dances with Harriet when no one else will. It is he who arrives at the Crown Inn in a carriage because such social nobodies as Miss Bates and her niece are in need of a ride. It is Mr. Knightley who marries Emma, not because she is the mistress of Hartfield and first lady of Highbury, but because she is finally a lovable human person.

The marriage of Emma to Mr. Knightley is the novel's culminating symbolic event. It can come only after Emma has put aside pretensions to superiority that are non-personal and after she has accepted reality as a condition for meaningful life. The structure of the novel is such that Emma encounters the meaning of reality and of person by seeing how impossible it is to ignore them. Gradually, Emma comes to see things as Mr. Knightley does, but their unity of vision comes only in the last volume of *Emma* (Chapters 37–55) when all of his predictions come true. Emma, who holds out against Mr. Knightley's view of life for two-thirds of the novel, is bent on proving her intuition superior to his judgments. Thus the novel develops with Emma attempting to bear the change of Miss Taylor's marriage by substituting Harriet Smith in her place, and beginning with Harriet, Emma initiates her attempt to mold reality to her view of it. All the while Mr. Knightley stands by and judges and predicts the course of events. The action of the novel, then, consists in a series of attempts on Emma's part to dominate the reality situation and to prove that because she is Miss Woodhouse of Hartfield and High-bury she is superior to all. More precisely, we can distinguish Emma's attempting to prove herself superior by remaking Harriet Smith, by refusing to acknowledge the personal worth of Jane Fairfax, and by accepting the challenge of Augusta Elton. Only after she carries on long enough to meet a series of humiliations from reality does Emma come to see the reality of herself. And in that vision she finds her finer character, if not her ulti-mate superiority. Only then does she see how invariably correct Mr. Knightley's interpretations of reality have been. Only then is she ready to be his wife.

The first volume of the novel (Chapters 1–18) dramatizes Emma's attempt to dominate by making Harriet Smith into a suitable wife for Mr. Elton. In the very first chapter Emma tells Mr. Knightley that she has been responsible for the Westons' marriage, that making marriages is "the greatest amusement in the world" (12), and that she will find a wife for Mr. Elton. Mr. Knightley's reply combines observation, judgment, and warning. To him the Westons are sensible people who have married without Emma's help: "You made a lucky guess; and *that* is all that can be said" (13). For him, "You are more likely

to have done harm to yourself, than good to them, by inter-.
ference'' (13). This observation is a prophecy, as is Mr. Knightley's remark about Mr. Elton: ''Depend upon it, a man of six or
seven-and-twenty can take care of himself'' (14). Emma needs
only Harriet to prove these statements true and to force from
Mr. Knightley further predictions on the course of events that
will be consequent upon her further abuse of reality.

Life with Mr. Woodhouse alone is neither intellectually nor
psychologically stimulating. Emma understands her father
completely and has fitted herself into his system. She knows
exactly how to care for him and she is unfailing in her sympathetic response to his daily perturbations. This is one quality
Emma never loses and her patience with her father and her
attachment to him are unfailing. Severe as are our judgments on
Emma for her many aberrations, they are always benign here.
Emma's sympathy for her father and his peculiarities elicit our
admiration at the same moment that her more creative and
fanciful efforts call forth harsh judgments. But Emma turns to
creativity precisely because her relation to her father allows her
none. Therefore when Harriet Smith arrives on the scene as ''the
natural daughter of somebody'' (22), Emma almost immediately
turns her into the daughter of a gentleman. Emma finds Harriet
exactly the person to help her to bear the change. She will make
Harriet into a suitable companion for Mr. Elton: ''It would be
an interesting, and certainly a very kind undertaking; highly
becoming her own situation in life, her leisure, and powers'' (24).

For Emma to make Harriet suitable for Mr. Elton she has to
make Robert Martin unsuitable for Harriet. There is more than
Harriet's welfare involved in this process of making and un-
making. To Emma, Harriet is ''useful.'' She is ''a valuable
addition to her privileges'' (26). Harriet presents no threat to
Emma, as Jane Fairfax and Mrs. Elton later do. Harriet adds to
Emma's privileges by showing how a friend of Miss Woodhouse
can be the bride of any gentleman. But for Harriet to marry

Martin would be for Harriet not only to lower herself, but to lower Miss Woodhouse as well. For Harriet to marry a man who is "so very clownish" (32) after having experienced the gentility of Mr. Woodhouse and Mr. Elton will not do at all.

The real problem that Emma does not sufficiently recognize is that Harriet is rather clownish herself. Mr. Knightley sees this immediately. He tells Mrs. Weston that the friendship of Harriet and Emma is a "bad thing." "I think they will neither of them do the other any good" (36). Harriet's ignorance can only flatter Emma's intelligence, and Emma's society can only put Harriet "out of conceit with all the other places she belongs to" (38). Therefore, when Emma begins to make Harriet into Mr. Elton's bride by denying her to Robert Martin, Mr. Knightley can only see her work as "nonsense, errant nonsense" (65). The two symbols of Emma's work in progress bear out Mr. Knightley's judgment of the reality.

The symbol of Emma's making Harriet into a lady suited to marry Highbury's gentleman-vicar is Emma's drawing Harriet's portrait. The taking of the portrait shows Emma making Harriet into someone other than herself.

> "Miss Woodhouse has given her friend the only beauty she wanted,"—observed Mrs. Weston to him [Mr. Elton]—not in the least suspecting that she was addressing a lover.—"The expression of the eye is most correct, but Miss Smith has not those eye-brows and eye-lashes. It is the fault of her face that she has them not."
>
> "Do you think so?" replied he. "I cannot agree with you. It appears to me a most perfect resemblance in every feature. I never saw such a likeness in my life. We must allow for the effect of shade, you know."
>
> "You have made her too tall, Emma," said Mr. Knightley.
>
> Emma knew that she had, but would not own it, and Mr. Elton warmly added,
>
> "Oh, no! certainly not too tall; not in the least too tall. Con-

sider, she is sitting down—which naturally presents a different—which in short gives exactly the idea—and the proportions must be preserved, you know. Proportions, fore-shortening—Oh, no! It gives one exactly the idea of such a height as Miss Smith's. Exactly so indeed!"

"It is very pretty," said Mr. Woodhouse. "So prettily done! Just as your drawings always are, my dear. I do not know any body who draws so well as you do . . ." (47–48).

Harriet does not have the height Emma gives her nor the eye-brows or eyelashes either. The tribute that is paid by the portrait is paid to the ingenuity of the artist, not to the beauty of the subject. As the picture suggests, Harriet is not the lady—not the gentleman's daughter suited to be a gentleman's wife—that Emma makes her. The inch or two that Emma adds to Harriet's stature is a literal symbol of Emma's attempt to raise the girl's social position. But Emma's improving nature by art is a botch. Mr. Elton responds only to the real Emma and, as his proposal to her shows, her artistic efforts in Harriet's behalf do neither young lady any good. Emma hurts both Harriet and herself and unwittingly proves her severest critic right. For Mr. Knightley had predicted that Emma and Harriet "will neither of them do the other any good."

The process of making Robert Martin less than he is follows immediately upon Emma's making Harriet more than she is. Robert Martin's letter arrives while Mr. Elton is carrying Harriet's picture to London to be framed. The real Harriet is left to face a real letter, but the reality is too distressing to Emma.

The style of the letter was much above her expectation. There were not merely no grammatical errors, but as a composition it would not have disgraced a gentleman; the language, though plain, was strong and unaffected, and the sentiments it conveyed very much to the credit of the writer. It was short, but expressed good sense, warm

attachment, liberality, propriety, even delicacy of feeling. She
paused over it, while Harriet stood anxiously watching for the
opinion, with a "Well, well," and was at last forced to add, "Is it a
good letter? or is it too short?"

"Yes, indeed, a very good letter," replied Emma rather slowly—
"so good a letter, Harriet, that every thing considered, I think one
of his sisters must have helped him. I can hardly imagine the young
man whom I saw talking with you the other day could express
himself so well, if left quite to his own powers, and yet it is not
the style of a woman; no, certainly, it is too strong and concise;
not diffuse enough for a woman. No doubt he is a sensible man, and
I suppose may have a natural talent for—thinks strongly and
clearly—and when he takes a pen in hand, his thoughts naturally
find proper words. It is so with some men. Yes, I understand the
sort of mind. Vigorous, decided, with sentiments to a certain point,
not coarse. A better written letter, Harriet, (returning it,) than I
had expected" (50–51).

Either Robert Martin's letter was written by his sister, as its
grammar and expression suggests, or he is a man with sentiments
to a certain point not coarse, but beyond that point . . . ?

Reality does no justice to Emma's prerogatives and power, as
Harriet herself and Martin's letter show. Therefore Harriet
becomes a portrait and the letter-writer becomes suspect: "It
would be a degradation" for Harriet to marry Martin. To Mr.
Knightley this is errant nonsense. He can only oppose what Emma
is doing to herself and others: "A degradation to illegitimacy and
ignorance, to be married to a respectable, intelligent gentleman-
farmer!" (62), he responds in indignation. Considering the
symbolic importance of marriage in Jane Austen's society, Emma
can have done nothing but harm to Harriet. "Till you chose to
turn her into a friend," says Mr. Knightley, "her mind had no
distaste for her own set, nor any ambition beyond it. . . . You
have been no friend to Harriet Smith, Emma" (63). Emma is not
yet convinced, however. She will not judge Harriet what she
finds her to be: "She knows now what gentlemen are; and nothing

but a gentleman in education and manner has any chance with Harriet" (65), Emma tells Mr. Knightley.

Emma has only to wait until she is alone in a carriage with Mr. Elton to find out how much of a gentleman he is. Then her "errant nonsense" is rewarded by Mr. Elton's "thick-headed nonsense" (134). Emma finds herself interrupted, "her subject cut up—her hand seized—her attention demanded, and Mr. Elton actually making violent love to her" (129). Mr. Knightleys' predictions come true: a man of twenty-six or twenty-seven will choose for himself, a woman who tries her hand at matchmaking is likely to put it in love's way, and Emma has been no friend to Harriet. It is no accident that Mr. Knightley appears in Chapters 1, 5, 7, and 12 to judge the reality and predict the course of action and its conclusion. He is the choric voice of reality that sounds on deaf ears. He comes and judges persons while Emma ignores individuals and tries to make and match social entities. But the Harriet that Emma raises is still very low, as Mr. Elton rudely reminds her: "Every body has their level" (132). The portrait that Emma creates is given the lie by the reality that Harriet is. The fault of Emma's pictorial art becomes the fault of her social art. Emma, who tries to present Harriet as the product of "her powers," finds that in her attempt to be superior by making Harriet superior she has sunk herself. When Mr. Elton proposed to her, she might well have answered him in his own words," Every body has their level." Emma learns something in the Harriet–Elton affair, but she has yet to learn that the superior person is the one who responds to character, not consequence. She has yet to learn that in Robert Martin there is true gentility and that in Jane Fairfax there is the young woman who deserves her regard. Mr. Knightley tells her both these things but only experience can make Emma understand them. The arrival of Jane Fairfax at the Bateses' and the delayed arrival of Frank Churchill at the Westons' sets that slow process of understanding in motion.

Mr. Knightley's conversation with Emma in Chapter 18 again defines the limits of expectation within which Frank Churchill will come to life. Emma and he argue about the meaning of Frank Churchill's delayed arrival: Why has he not yet come to pay his father and step-mother a wedding visit? Emma argues that the Churchills prevent him:

> "The Churchills are very likely in fault," said Mr. Knightley, coolly; "but I dare say he might come if he would."
>
> "I do not know why you should say so. He wishes exceedingly to come; but his uncle and aunt will not spare him."
>
> "I cannot believe that he has not the power of coming, if he made a point of it. It is too unlikely, for me to believe it without proof" (145).

To Mr. Knightley, Frank is old enough, man enough, and independent enough not to be without fault in neglecting the Westons: "There is one thing, Emma, which a man can always do, if he chuses, and that is, his duty . . ." (146). Frank Churchill cannot be "really amiable" and cannot have a true "delicacy towards the feelings of other people" (149). The perceptive reader who has seen Mr. Knightley plot the course of events in Emma's relation to Harriet can hardly ignore his words here. One has only to await the arrival of Frank Churchill to see them come true. But Frank cannot arrive without Jane Fairfax, and it is precisely his relation to Jane that brings Mr. Knightley's judgment of him to life.

Now if Mr. Knightley does not like Frank Churchill, Emma does not like Jane Fairfax. The difference is that Mr. Knightley finds Frank in want of merit; whereas Emma finds Jane too good. One judges, the other is jealous. Mr. Knightley states Emma's unconscious relation to Jane precisely: Emma "saw in her the really accomplished young woman, which she wanted to be thought herself" (166).

Emma decides, however, that she will be particularly good to Jane Fairfax during her stay at the Bateses'. Yes, she will be good to Jane in spite of the fact that before the girl arrives she suspects her of being in love with Mr. Dixon. But Emma's good wishes are short-lived and an affair of kinds between Jane and Dixon is just too tempting. One evening at Hartfield kills Emma's good resolutions:

> They had music; Emma was obliged to play; and the thanks and praise which necessarily followed appeared to her an affectation of candour, an air of greatness, meaning only to shew off in higher style her [Jane's] own very superior performance. She was, besides, which was the the worst of all, so cold, so cautious! There was no getting at her real opinion. Wrapt up in a cloak of politeness, she seemed determined to hazard nothing. She was disgustingly, was suspiciously reserved (168–169).

Jane is especially reserved about the Dixons. "It did her no service however. Her caution was thrown away. Emma saw its artifice, and returned to her first surmises" (169). The arrival of Frank Churchill, who knows both Jane and Dixon, gives Emma a confidant and the affair becomes a favorite topic of conversation between them.

Emma cherishes her position in Highbury society and the second volume (Chapters 19–36) shows this very clearly. The dinner that is given by the Coles is in every way satisfactory to Emma. First of all, she feels that her position in society is so much above theirs that they would not dare to invite her: "they ought to be taught that it was not for them to arrange the terms on which the superior families would visit them" (207). Then she feels that it would be nice to have an invitation: "She felt that she should like to have had the power of refusal" (208). Next Emma fears that she will not be invited to a party that all her friends are attending. That anxiety is allayed, however; Emma is invited and she triumphs: "She was received with a cordial respect which could not but please, and given all the consequence she could wish for" (214). There are other instances of Emma's superiority being flattered besides the Coles' dinner.

Mr. Weston's proposal of a dance, Frank Churchill tells Emma,
"waits only your approbation to be acted upon" (250). Emma is
the sovereign of Highbury and very much enjoys the power of
scepter. Consequently, Mrs. Weston's making a match between
Mr. Knightley and Jane Fairfax entirely distresses her: "she could
not at all endure the idea of Jane Fairfax at Donwell Abbey. A
Mrs. Knightley for them all to give way to!" (228)

But even before Mrs. Weston snatches a page from Emma's
book of perquisites and takes to matchmaking, Jane Fairfax is a
danger. "Jane Fairfax was very elegant, remarkably elegant; and
she had herself the highest value for elegance" (167). Jane Fairfax is clearly a personal threat to Emma Woodhouse. That is
why the latter is so quick to invent a lover for her in the person
of the married Mr. Dixon. This attribution immediately enables
Emma to see herself in a moral position superior to Jane's.
Emma's wish to be personally superior makes Jane morally
inferior. It is an old story all over again:

> Pride measures her prosperity not by her own goods but by others'
> wants. Pride would not deign to be a goddess, if there were no
> inferiors she could rule and triumph over. Her happiness shines
> brightly only in comparison to others' misery, and their poverty
> binds them and hurts them the more as her wealth is displayed.
> Pride is the infernal serpent that steals into the hearts of men,
> thwarting and holding them back from choosing the better way of
> life.[18]

It is well to note that Emma almost put by this fantasy about
Jane and Dixon, but as soon as Jane sat down to the pianoforte
and showed herself Miss Woodhouse's superior, Emma
found her "suspiciously reserved" and "returned to her first
surmises." Jane's pianoforte, of course, is extremely important
in this section of the novel. It is as symbolic of Emma's relation
to Jane as the portrait is of Emma's relation to Harriet earlier in
the novel. The pianoforte is the instrument at which Jane Fairfax

excells; hers is the "very superior performance." When Jane plays, all the elegance that characterizes her comes together in music. And Emma is incapable of duplicating that kind of harmony, for she is not as accomplished as Jane Fairfax. Therefore, the pianoforte is bearable to Emma only as a symbol of Jane's inferiority: "I can see it in no other light than as an offering of love," says Emma (219). As a mysterious gift, it can only have come from Mr. Dixon, Jane's lover. The pianoforte proves to Emma not Jane's superiority, as it should, but the very opposite.

But Emma cannot ignore Mrs. Elton as easily as she does Jane Fairfax when the vicar's redoubtable wife appears on the Highbury scene. Mrs. Elton is a threat to Emma's composure because she married the man Emma had assigned to Harriet. Therefore, "Emma had feelings, less of curiosity than of pride or propriety, to make her resolve on not being the last to pay her respects" to Mr. Elton's wife (270). Emma finds Mrs. Elton to want elegance after she visits her at the parsonage. Clearly then Mrs. Elton does not pose the same kind of problem to Emma that Jane Fairfax, who is so completely elegant, does. Rather, Mrs. Elton represents the threat of an all-encompassing vulgarity. When she visits Hartfield and sprinkles her conversation with "Maple Grove" and "barouche-landau," "Knightley" and "caro sposo," she offends Emma's sense of decorum. When she goes on to find that Mrs. Weston, in spite of her having once been Emma's governess, is a "gentlewoman" and "lady-like" (278), when she discovers Mr. Knightley to be "quite the gentleman" (278–279), when she offers to have Emma introduced into Bath society, when she proposes remedies for Mr. Woodhouse's ills, and when she suggests that she and Emma found a musical circle—when Mrs. Elton does these things in the Woodhouse parlor, Emma finds the "dignity of Miss Woodhouse, of Hartfield, . . . sunk indeed!" (279). The next time Emma Woodhouse and Augusta Elton meet we learn that "a state of warfare" exists between them (282). The victory is ultimately Emma's, but the fight is bitter because

Mrs. Elton is a bride. And "a bride, you know, my dear," says Mr. Woodhouse to his daughter, "is always first in company, let others be who they may" (280).

With the appearance of Mrs. Elton, Jane Austen introduces into the novel its last major symbol, the bride. This symbol is presently to apply to Harriet Smith, Jane Fairfax, and Emma, herself, just as it immediately applies to Mrs. Elton. Its complexity is suggested by the range of characters it touches, and one facet of that complexity is revealed by Mrs. Elton, who as a bride threatens that easy domination of others that was found to be Emma's in her relation to Harriet and Jane. Mrs. Elton as "first in company" becomes a grotesque reflection of Emma's love of social sovereignty when she attempts to bring Miss Woodhouse, as just one of the company, under her rule. Besides patronizing Emma when she returns the wedding visit at Hartfield, Mrs. Elton almost immediately usurps Emma's perquisites in Highbury society. Events at the Crown Inn, Donwell Abbey, and Box Hill make this evident.

The ball at the Crown Inn is planned by the Westons and Frank Churchill to honor Emma. But she is made to give way to Mrs. Elton:

> It had just occurred to Mrs. Weston that Mrs. Elton must be asked to begin the ball; that she would expect it; which interfered with all their wishes of giving Emma that distinction.—Emma heard the sad truth with fortitude. . . . Emma must submit to stand second to Mrs. Elton, though she always considered the ball as peculiarly for her (325).

Besides taking precedence, Mrs. Elton takes revenge: she and her husband decide to humiliate Harriet and in the process to offend Emma. Mr. Elton refuses to dance with Harriet, his wife encourages him "by significant glances" (327), and Emma "would not look again. Her heart was in a glow, and she feared her face might be as hot" (328). Mrs. Elton makes another bid for prominence when Mr. Knightley halfheartedly proposes a strawberry party at Donwell Abbey: "Only give me a carte-blanche.—I am Lady Patroness, you know," she says to him. "It is my party. Leave it all to me. I will invite your guests" (354). At Box Hill, an outing which she first proposed, Mrs. Elton once again challenges Emma's position in society. She refuses to acknowledge Frank Churchill's assumption that Emma, "wherever she is, presides." Indeed, "Mrs. Elton swelled at the idea of Miss Woodhouse's presiding." She sets herself up as "the *Chaperon* of the party," and quickly agrees with her husband when he says, "Every body knows what is due to *you*" (369–370).

As a bride, then, Mrs. Elton unquestionably is a clear and present threat to Emma's casually assumed preeminence. She touches Emma at a more personal level, too, precisely because she is a married woman. The wife of Philip Elton shows Emma how wrong she was about the clergyman's gentility and reminds her how silly she was in thinking that Mr. Elton would distinguish Harriet as his wife. Mrs. Elton takes to patronizing Jane Fairfax, too. This very selection of Jane reminds Emma of her own shabby treatment of the girl. And what Mrs. Elton attempts to do by way of managing Jane Fairfax' future serves as a suitable reflector of Emma's manipulation of the simple Harriet. All round, then, Mrs. Elton is a piquant unpleasantry on the Highbury landscape, at least as far as Emma is concerned.

The sudden announcement that Jane Fairfax is to be the bride of Frank Churchill leads Emma to canvass more completely her neglect of Jane, so different from Mrs. Elton's painful attentions to her. Jane Fairfax as the bride of Frank Churchill is a revelation of injustice to Emma: of her own injustice to Jane and of Frank's to herself. The symbol of the pianoforte is reintroduced, and Emma finds that Frank sent the instrument, not Mr. Dixon. He did not go to London to get a haircut to please Emma; he went to buy a musical instrument to please Jane. Frank never loved

Emma; he used her to hide his engagement of Jane. Miss Fairfax
is guilty of no affair with a married man. Her much bruited
reserve is simply the secrecy imposed on her by engagement to
Churchill. Jane, whom Emma has disliked and neglected,
emerges as "a girl of . . . steadiness of character and good judgment" (400). Frank, whom Emma has distinguished and defended
is found guilty of "horrible indelicacy" (397): "What right had
he to come among us with affection and faith engaged, and with
manners so *very* disengaged?" (396). Jane's reserve has been
better than Frank's lack of it.

Before he had ever met him and judging from the facts at hand,
Mr. Knightley had said, in Chapter 18, that "there is one thing
. . . which a man can always do, if he chuses, and that is, his
duty . . ." (146). The suffering that Frank has caused Jane and
the embarrassment he has caused Emma have justified this conclusion, and when Jane is revealed as Frank's bride-to-be, Mr.
Knightley's suspicion, which followed on the game with the
children's blocks, is realized: there is "something of private
liking, of private understanding even, between Frank Churchill
and Jane" (344). In every way that she looks at the Churchill–
Fairfax engagement, Emma finds herself wrong and Mr. Knightley
right. Jane Fairfax' future happiness proves to be Emma's
present humiliation. Jane as Frank's bride-to-be becomes a
vision of reality for the fanciful Emma.

One thing that Emma sees clearly is that Harriet cannot marry
the man engaged to Jane. Emma's reading of events has again
proved incorrect. She was as wrong in hoping to match Harriet
and Frank as Mrs. Weston was in hoping to match Frank and
Emma. Men of three-and-twenty, as well as those of six or seven-
and-twenty, will choose for themselves. But Emma also learns
that girls of seventeen can be willful too. Harriet comes to Emma
and projects herself as the bride of Mr. Knightley. Emma is
abashed because "it darted through her, with the speed of an
arrow, that Mr. Knightley must marry no one but herself!"

(408). But it was Emma who said to Mr. Knightley, in Chapter 8, "Oh! Harriet may pick and choose. Were you, yourself, ever to marry, she is the very woman for you" (64). Now that Harriet has decided to pick and choose Emma realizes the egregious error she has made in singling out Miss Smith: "But Harriet was less humble, had fewer scruples than formerly. . . . If Harriet, from being humble, were grown vain, it was her doing too" (414). Harriet has come to believe in Emma's portrait of her. And in seeing what she has done, Emma comes to realize in her life the perfect justice of the words of Swift:

> When a Man's fancy gets *astride* on his Reason, when Imagination is at Cuffs with the senses, and common Understanding, as well as common Sense, is Kickt out of Doors; the first Proselyte he makes, is Himself, and when that is once compass'd, the Difficulty is not so great in bringing over others.[19]

With Harriet Smith wanting to marry the man Emma loves, it is quite clear that Emma has brought over another.

Fortunately for Emma, Harriet is not a very steadfast individual. A few weeks in London and another proposal from Robert Martin suffice to erase the image of Mr. Knightley. They suffice, too, to suggest how really ephemeral Emma's portrait of Harriet was. Because when Harriet becomes the bride of Martin, she is taken to Abbey-Mill farm, where some months before her measure had been accurately taken: "In that very room she had been measured last September, with her two friends. There were the pencilled marks and memorandums on the wainscot by the window. *He* had done it" (187). Emma had made Harriet taller than she really was and symbolically raised her in social rank by giving her the stature of a lady. The consequences were repeatedly disastrous. Robert Martin had taken Harriet's measure exactly and accepted her for herself. Emma's contribution to Harriet— besides curing her of "her school-girl's giggle" (58)—has been nothing more than making her take a rather circuitous route to happiness at Abbey-Mill farm. Harriet as Robert Martin's bride stands as a reality that Emma cannot tamper with. What she has already done to Harriet can only suggest the justice of Mr. Knightley's remark, "You have been no friend to Harriet Smith, Emma" (63).

But if Emma has been mistaken about Harriet and about Jane, she has been most mistaken about herself. Emma finds herself her own worst creation. The Emma who decides that no one but herself must marry Mr. Knightley is the same Emma who once decided "that if she *were* to marry," Frank Churchill "was the very person to suit her in age, character and condition" (119). Emma, who has set up for understanding, finds everything in a muddle: wrong about Philip Elton and wrong about Frank Churchill, wrong about Jane and wrong about Harriet, wrong about Martin and wrong about Dixon. But most of all wrong about Emma Woodhouse. Mrs. Weston's idea that Mr. Knightley liked Jane Fairfax enough to marry her annoyed Emma, but not simply because she did not want to give way to a Mrs. Knightley. Harriet's declaration of love makes Emma find an equally valid and more portentous reason in her own love for George Knightley. Emma, who thought she once loved Frank Churchill, directly denies that she ever loved him the moment she finds Mr. Knightley lurking in Harriet's heart. Emma never loved anyone but Mr. Knightley, but she was so preoccupied shaping others and making matches for them that she never noticed that Mr. Knightley was shaping her to be the woman who would be the perfect match for himself.

With Emma in doubt about Mr. Knightley's affection, she is haunted by the Crown Inn ball, the Donwell strawberry party, and the Box Hill excursion. Mr. Knightley and Harriet danced at the Inn; they walked and talked alone at the Abbey. At Box Hill Emma remembers so exasperating Mr. Knightley by her treatment of Miss Bates that he brought himself to reprimand her so severely that she cried. These three places where Mrs. Elton was so prominent and Emma so humiliated threaten to preserve Mrs. Elton's importance by preventing Emma from ever becoming Mrs. Knightley. As the rain and wind add to the unpleasantness, Emma's thoughts again turn to the evening of the day of the Weston marriage:

> It reminded her of their first forlorn tête-à-tête, on the evening of Mrs. Weston's wedding-day; but Mr. Knightley had walked in then, soon after tea, and dissipated every melancholy fancy. Alas! such delightful proofs of Hartfield's attraction, as those sort of visits conveyed, might shortly be over (422).
>
> Mr. Knightley to be no longer coming there for his evening comfort!—No longer walking in at all hours, as if ever willing to change his own home for their's!—How was it to be endured? (422)

But as the sun appears the next day and summer returns, Mr. Knightley comes to console Emma on her losing Churchill, finds that she does not love Frank, and declares his own affection:

> He had found her agitated and low.—Frank Churchill was a villain.—He heard her declare that she had never loved him. Frank Churchill's character was not desperate.—She was his own Emma, by hand and word, when they returned into the house; and if he could have thought of Frank Churchill then, he might have deemed him a very good sort of fellow (433).

By the time Mr. Knightley's proposal occurs, Emma has changed considerably. She has judged herself severely:

> With insufferable vanity had she believed herself in the secret of everybody's feelings; with unpardonable arrogance proposed to arrange everybody's destiny. She was proved to have been universally mistaken; and she had not quite done nothing—for she had done mischief. She had brought evil on Harriet, on herself, and she too much feared, on Mr. Knightley (412–413).

Even before Mr. Knightley declares his love, Emma has resolved upon reform:

the only source whence any thing like consolation or composure could be drawn, was in the resolution of her own better conduct, and the hope that, however inferior in spirit and gaiety might be the following and every future winter of her life to the past, it would yet find her more rational, more acquainted with herself, and leave her less to regret when it were gone (423).

The new Emma is now ready to supersede Mrs. Elton and become a bride who deserves to be first in company.

It is one of the nice ironies of the novel that Emma does not succeed in dominating either Harriet Smith or Jane Fairfax. Harriet turns out to be more real than Emma's portrait of her and Martin's letter is found to be very much like Mr. Knightley's proposal to Emma, for both are cast "in plain, unaffected gentle-man-like English" (448). Jane is revealed as "one of the most lovely and accomplished young women in England" (400) and as better than both Emma and Frank: "There is a likeness in our destiny," Emma tells Churchill, "the destiny which bids fair to connect us with two characters so much superior to our own" (478). The only one whom Emma succeeds in overcoming is Mrs. Elton, who snubbed Harriet, patronized Jane, and insulted Emma. Emma's engagement to George Knightley augurs the end of Mrs. Elton's prominence: "No more exploring parties to Donwell made for her. Oh! no; there would be a Mrs. Knightley to throw cold water on everything" (469).

Emma did not allow Harriet and Jane to be themselves during most of her acquaintance with them. The portrait and the piano-forte as symbols of her attitude toward them obstructed her vision of the reality of each of the young women. Only Harriet's threat to Emma's own personal happiness was sufficient to make her see how justly Miss Smith's measure had been taken by Robert Martin. Only Frank Churchill's preference of Jane Fairfax to herself could make Emma recognize the merit of the girl to whom Frank is totally devoted. Emma, however, saw Mrs. Elton clearly from the first moment of their meeting, even though the vicar's wife approached Emma under the conventional cover provided her as a bride. Her status as bride stood between her vulgarity and Emma's attempts to prevent her from asserting it. But only after Emma no longer reflected Augusta Elton's will to power in herself did she deserve Mr. Knightley's proposal. Emma's status as bride then is the outward confirmation of an inner change and is not merely an adornment of power. When Emma is truly ready to become Mrs. Knightley, then she is ready to be "first in company." Unlike Mrs. Elton, Emma has come "to understand, thoroughly understand her own heart" (412). Emma as a bride asks to be seen as a person who has found herself as truly as she has found the persons of Harriet Smith and Jane Fairfax revealed in their marriages to Robert Martin and Frank Churchill.

When one reads the novel in this way he can clearly see how Jane Austen displaces one pattern of values for another as the character of Emma develops. He can also see Emma's change in understanding, attitude, and conduct registered in her changing sense of the meaning of the words "true gentility." In recording Emma's movement toward a meaningful life, Jane Austen shows her heroine gradually recognizing true gentility to be a matter of intrinsic human worth, not of depersonalizing social rank and power. Indeed, the action and symbols in the novel enforce a reading of such a change in Emma's understanding.

As soon as Emma meets Harriet she endows her with gentility:

> "There can scarcely be a doubt that her father is a gentleman—and a gentleman of fortune.—Her allowance is very liberal; nothing has ever been grudged for her improvement or comfort.—That she is a gentleman's daughter, is indubitable to me; that she associates with gentlemen's daughters, no one, I apprehend, will deny" (62).

By giving Harriet dignity of birth and association, Emma makes her a suitable substitute for Miss Taylor, who married into a

family "rising into gentility" (15). Robert Martin is not suited
to marry Harriet because he is not gently born. He is not her
"equal," Emma tells Mr. Knightley (61). Even though his letter
of proposal "would not have disgraced a gentleman" (51), he is
not a Mr. Elton, who seems to have "grown particularly
gentle of late" and whose manners have "more gentleness" than
Mr. Knightley's (34). On the contrary,

> "[his] appearance is so much against him, and his manner so bad, that
> if she [Harriet] ever were disposed to favour him, she is not now.
> . . . She knows now what gentlemen are; and nothing but a gentle-
> man in education and manner has any chance with Harriet,"

Emma tells Mr. Knightley (65).

Emma has given Harriet a gentleman for father, has put her in
the company of the ever-so-gentle Mr. Woodhouse and the ever-
so-polite Mr. Elton, and has made her the companion of a gentleman's daughter. Emma values Mr. Elton as a gentleman because
of his education, manner, and position. She objects to Robert
Martin, a gentleman-farmer, on the opposite grounds. Her
criteria for gentility have nothing to do with personal integrity
and good judgment. Mr. Knightley seems to value little else:
"Robert Martin's manners have sense, sincerity, and good-
humour to recommend them; and his mind has more true
gentility than Harriet Smith could understand" (65).

The novel pits Emma's sense of true gentility against Mr.
Knightley's. Hers leads her to draw an inaccurate portrait; his, to
criticize it. Hers leads her to criticize Martin's letter; his,
Harriet's refusal. Emma pays the price of Mr. Elton's nonsense.
Robert Martin, who symbolically took Harriet's measure
exactly, proves his true gentility and marries her. His grammatical letter showed more gentility and good sense than Harriet's
refusal, which Emma was forced to write for her ungrammatical
friend. Emma finally sees Robert Martin's estimate of Harriet as a
true one and she finally accepts Mr. Knightley's description of
Martin as a man of true gentility:

as Emma became acquainted with Robert Martin, who was now introduced at Hartfield, she fully acknowledged in him all the appearance of sense and worth which could bid fairest for her little friend (482).

Emma's problem with Jane Fairfax is that Jane has too much gentility. Though Jane is an orphan, there is no question about her parents: their marriage "had had its day of fame and pleasure, hope and interest" (163). Jane herself has all the excellence of the daughter of a gentleman: "Jane Fairfax was elegant, remarkably elegant; and she had herself the highest value for elegance." Hers was

> a style of beauty, of which elegance was the reigning character, and as such, she [Emma] must, in honour, by all her principles, admire it:—elegance, which, whether of person or of mind, she saw so little in Highbury (167).

Jane Fairfax is Harriet's superior and Emma's equal, but Emma will have little to do with her. Emma treats her as Miss Bates's niece—as socially too low to be seriously noticed. She invents the Dixon affair and the pianoforte as its love offering to make her as much morally below her as she is socially. In doing so Emma finds nothing vulgar in herself. But Jane Austen suggests Emma's corresponding lack of elegance. She has Emma flirt with the man Jane is engaged to, which counterpoints in truth Emma's fiction of a Jane–Dixon affair. Also, Emma is made to insult Miss Bates, to whom Jane is never rude, no matter how much provoked.

All the while Mr. Knightley sees Jane's true gentility. She is "the really accomplished young woman," which Emma wanted to be thought herself. Jane's pianoforte, therefore, which so troubles Emma, signifies accomplishment to Mr. Knightley. Jane's engagement to Frank Churchill is to Mr. Knightley nothing less than Churchill's good fortune:

> ". . . Frank Churchill is, indeed, the favourite of fortune. Every thing turns out for his good.—He meets with a young woman at a

watering-place, gains her affection, cannot even weary her by negligent treatment—and had he and all his family sought round the world for a perfect wife for him, they could not have found her superior . . .'' (428).

Emma finally agrees with Mr. Knightley, and goes so far as to rank Jane with him and above herself when she speaks to Churchill of them as "two characters so much superior to our own.'' This is only a fair evaluation, for Frank, the gentleman, and Emma, the lady, treated Jane Fairfax with the utmost want of true gentility. For her part, Jane showed the worth of her character by her breaking the engagement with Frank and by refusing to be patronized by Emma. That Frank gains her as a wife and Emma as a friend is more to their personal advantage than Jane's.

Emma's encounter with Mrs. Elton is a battle for social position. The combatants are unevenly matched. There is no question of Emma's superior gentility, no question of her superior intelligence and civility. Mrs. Elton's only immediate advantage is that she is a bride, and that advantage also soon becomes Emma's. But Emma does not become Mrs. Knightley until she realizes her ungentle conduct towards Robert Martin, Harriet, Jane, and Miss Bates. Until she is able to find personal value in them, she is unable to know herself. Until she is able to see true gentility in Martin and until she realizes that a Miss Bates deserves the apology of a Miss Woodhouse, she is unable to realize what gentility requires of her as a gentlewoman. Once Emma knows herself and others, she is ready to accept the responsibility of the bride of George Knightley.

"The inner logic of the work suffices for all the moral implications and it is the reader's task to draw the right conclusions from its outcome,'' wrote Baudelaire.[20] The action and symbols of *Emma* show the heroine attempting to live meaningfully in her world by applying a lethal measure of social acceptability to the people she meets. Her understanding of the meaning of gentility is opposed by George Knightley, who insists that Emma recognize personal and individual goodness and accomplishment as the keynotes of true gentility. After resisting in every way she knows how, Emma can resist no longer, She acquiesces in reality, learns experientially the meaning of true gentility, and symbolically overcomes the last representative of the social measure of individual worth, Augusta Elton. The novel ends by affirming in a marriage the importance of human relationships based on personal worth and by debunking a univocal social standard of false gentility:

> The wedding was very much like other weddings, where the parties have no taste for finery or parade; and Mrs. Elton, from the particulars detailed by her husband, thought it all extremely shabby, and very inferior to her own—"Very little white satin, very few lace veils; a most pitiful business!—Selina would stare when she heard of it."—But, in spite of these deficiences, the wishes, the hopes, the confidence, the predictions of the small band of true friends who witnessed the ceremony, were fully answered in the perfect happiness of the union (484).

The marriage shows that Emma has accepted the Knightley pattern for true gentility as the norm for a meaningful personal life. That pattern displaces the one upheld by Mrs. Elton, who adheres to finery and parade as the measure of life's meaning. The happiness of the Knightleys and the bitterness of the Eltons suggests which pattern develops the better person.

"The imagination," wrote Kierkegaard,

> is what providence uses in order to get men into reality, into existence, to get them far enough out, or in, or down in existence. And when the imagination has helped them as far out as they are meant to go—that is where reality, properly speaking, begins.[21]

Emma rushes down the road of life on the hobby-horse of imagination and crashes into the hard wall of reality. She is forcibly made to realize that she can truly be herself only if she allows other persons to be themselves. The real Harriet is less vivid than the Harriet she created; the real Jane is superior to the one Emma invented. Once Emma allows them their true person-alities, she can find her own. Once she allows the totality of reality to dictate her conduct, she can put by fanciful constructs and turn to accurate judgments. Emma's judgments in the face of truth become as credible as Mr. Knightley's. The effort and promise of the future will be to keep them that way:

> "What had she to wish for? Nothing, but to grow more worthy of him, whose intentions and judgment had been ever so superior to her own. Nothing, but that the lessons of her past folly might teach her humility and circumspection in future" (475).

The guarantee of Emma's good resolutions is Mr. Knightley's taking her as his wife. The novel comes round on itself as its ending returns to Mr. Woodhouse, Emma, and Mr. Knightley at Hartfield. But the danger of egoism has given way to the truth of love. Emma has moved from the side of her father to that of her husband. The girl who began the novel as Miss Woodhouse ends it as Mrs. Knightley. Jane Austen suggests in the last chapter of *Emma* a return to the tableau of the first chapter,[22] but she asks us to recognize that the meaning of the symbol has changed: the whole of the novel suggests that the subtraction of one Woodhouse and the addition of a second Knightley has made more than a nominal change in the sum of reality and happiness at Hartfield.

6

Dignity and Duty in *Persuasion*

On Monday, October 11th, 1813, Jane Austen wrote to her sister Cassandra, "I am looking over Self-Control again, & my opinion is confirmed of its being an excellently-meant, elegantly-written Work, without anything of Nature or Probability in it. I declare I do not know whether Laura's passage down the American River, is not the most natural, possible, everyday thing she ever does."[1] Critics have been less ironic in ruminating on the nature and probability of at least two incidents in *Persuasion*. Mrs. Smith and Dick Musgrove have given all readers some cause for wonder.

Jane Austen is certainly avoiding chiaroscuro when she has Mrs. Smith sketch a character in bold lines:

> ". . . Mr. Elliot is a man without heart or conscience; a designing, wary, cold-blooded being, who thinks only of himself; who, for his own interest or ease, would be guilty of any cruelty, or any treachery, that could be perpetrated without risk of his general character. He has no feeling for others. Those whom he has been the chief cause of leading into ruin, he can neglect and desert without the smallest compunction. He is totally beyond the reach of any sentiment of justice or compassion. Oh! he is black at heart, hollow and black!"[2]

The reader will here recognize Mrs. Smith putting the dying William Elliot to the ax for Anne Elliot's benefit. But a natural death would have seemed more appropriate.

Before this revelation takes place, Anne has decided against William Elliot. Drawing on the maturity of her feelings and judgment, Anne has rejected Lady Russell's second attempt at persuasion and with it rejected what marriage to William Elliot offers her:

> The charm of Kellynch and of "Lady Elliot" all faded away. She never could accept him. And it was not only that her feelings were still adverse to any man save one; her judgment, on a serious consideration of the possibilities of such a case, was against Mr. Elliot (160).

After this moment of decision and the analysis that immediately follows it, Mrs. Smith's exposure seems unnecessary. Anne's sigh of relief subsequent to it seems forced: "It was just possible that she might have been persuaded by Lady Russell" (211). The action of the novel prior to Mrs. Smith's revelation, as we have just seen, has already denied the possibility of Anne's being persuaded.

Robert Liddell has complained that "No part of the novel has caused greater dissatisfaction than the story of Mrs. Smith."[3] This is only one of many objections. Marvin Mudrick finds that Mrs. Smith's "presence is too useful, her story too pat in its corroboration of Anne."[4] Elizabeth Jenkins finds Mrs. Smith "a piece of machinery which has not been softened into life."[5] W. A. Craik takes up the image:

> Mrs. Smith is a difficulty; she comes too late, is obviously a convenient piece of machinery, and having too much to reveal in too little time, in a novel where by Jane Austen's standards characters say little, she talks too much.[6]

With Mrs. Smith, says Mary Lascelles, Jane Austen "succumbed to the state of fatigue in which mistakes are made."[7]

The introduction of "poor Dick" Musgrove has caused similar regret. Craik finds it a "notorious example of Jane Austen's dissociating herself from her characters."[8] Jane Austen's comment on Mrs. Musgrove's "large fat sighings" is found "inadmissable" by Jenkins.[9] Trilling regrets it as a "unique lapse"

into "aesthetic-spiritual snobbery."[10] And Mudrick asks, "Why
are Mrs. Musgrove and her son so ill treated?"[11] For him,
"Neither Mrs. Musgrove nor her son illustrates anything except
the author's exasperation with both."[12] There seems to be some
just cause for annoyance here for another reason too. The business
of Dick Musgrove is not necessary to the cause-effect relationship between the Musgroves and Captain Wentworth. He is well
established in their midst before it appears. Like Mrs. Smith,
Dick Musgrove seems an obtrusion on the plot of *Persuasion*.
Can anything be said in their favor?

Robert Liddell has not been as offended as some by Jane
Austen's handling of the Musgroves, mother and son. "The stage
sorrow of obese opera-singers is a perennial joke."[13] Mrs.
Musgrove's sighing over poor Dick is something of the same
kind, especially when one considers the object of her sorrow.

> . . . The Musgroves had had the ill fortune of a very troublesome,
> hopeless son; and the good fortune to lose him before he reached
> his twentieth year; . . . he had been sent to sea, because he was
> stupid and unmanageable on shore; . . . he had been very little
> cared for at any time by his family, though quite as much as he
> deserved; seldom heard of, and scarcely at all regretted, when the
> intelligence of his death abroad had worked its way to Uppercross,
> two years before.
>
> He had, in fact, . . . been nothing better than a thick-headed,
> unfeeling, unprofitable Dick Musgrove, who had never done any
> thing to entitle himself to more than the abbreviation of his name,
> living or dead (50–51).

What the narrator seems to be scoring in the incident is its in-
congruity. When Dick was alive, no one much cared for him.
Having died, everyone cares for him: "his sisters were now doing
all they could for him, by calling him 'poor Richard,' " and his
mother by regretting the loss of a son destined to be another
Captain Wentworth. The situation strikes Jane Austen as ridiculous, and she says so. ". . . A person as sensitive as Jane Austen

. . . is far more likely to make a ruthless remark than many people with thicker skins," remarks Liddell.[14]

This is not a complete vindication, of course, because Dick's second death at the narrator's hand is not causally related to the plot, as I have already indicated. But it is an instance of the narrator's speaking loudly and boldly and asking to be heard. And what is said points to the heart of *Persuasion*. The Musgroves' grief is false grief because it is inspired by an unworthy object. Dick Musgrove was "troublesome," "unmanageable," "thick-headed," "unfeeling," and "unprofitable"; "he had never done anything to entitle himself to more than the abbreviation of his name." That the natural son and brother of the Musgroves should be mourned is one thing. That he should become his mother's Captain Wentworth and call forth "large fat sighings" and that he should become his sisters' "poor Richard" is another. The narrator insists that if there is no proportion between grief and love—"he had been very little cared for at any time by his family"—there should at least be a proportion between grief and worth. Dick Musgrove was frankly an unworthy son. There was in him no true dignity to call forth tear-floods and sigh-tempests. *Persuasion* "subjects to ironical scrutiny some of the most portentous facts of human existence," writes Joseph Duffy,[15] and Dick Musgrove is a touchstone of one of them. "The real dignity of a man lies not in what he *has*, but in what he *is*."[16] Dick *has* the name Musgrove, but he *is* unworthy of his family's grief.

The theme of *Persuasion* is the relationship between dignity (from *dignus* meaning worth or merit) and duty. To be a person of true dignity one has to be dutiful. If family relationships break down, as in the case of the Musgroves and Dick, one has to be worthy in spite of neglect. ". . . The deepest impression we carry away from *Persuasion* is one of human isolation,"[17] says Walton Litz. Both Dick Musgrove and Anne Elliot are isolated from family affection, but the difference between Anne and Dick is that she achieves a true dignity in her aloneness and he does not because she is dutiful and he is not. Dick's life is the anti-model of true human dignity in *Persuasion*. No wonder he "is exhumed from his undeserved sanctification" and made the target of "the author's exasperation."[18]

William Elliot is also a man without true dignity. He has the name of Elliot, he has pleasing manners, he has a large fortune; but he is a fraud. The man who is the heir to Kellynch-hall and a suitor to the consequence of Sir Walter and Elizabeth, once wrote of them:

> "Give me joy: I have got rid of Sir Walter and Miss. They are gone back to Kellynch, and almost made me swear to visit them this summer, but my first visit to Kellynch will be with a surveyor, to tell me how to bring it with best advantage to the hammer" (203).

William Elliot's attentions to Anne are motivated by his desire to keep "Sir Walter single by the watchfulness which a son-in-law's rights would have given" (250). Mrs. Smith's revelation of William Elliot's character shows him to be an unworthy individual, a person who scorns duty and has no dignity. Paul Zeitlow, in his excellent essay on *Persuasion*, suggests that "Mrs. Smith is something like a goddess who descends on stage at a crucial moment to avert catastrophe."[19] Since Anne seems determined against William Elliot before Mrs. Smith's revelation, this strikes me as an overstatement. But it does emphasize the rather spectacular way Jane Austen takes to make the rift between Anne's true dignity and Elliot's lack of it unmistakable.

Whatever reasons prevented Jane Austen from assimilating Mrs. Smith and Dick Musgrove into the plot of *Persuasion* with a greater nicety seem to be forever lost to us. As Mudrick says, "Here is the book, and as it is we must judge it."[20] My judgment is that these two episodes that have been so much objected to have a salience that makes them esthetically unsatisfying. But that they clearly point to the main theme of *Persuasion* does suggest why they are there. They are episodes that do not fit quite comfortably into a plot which they nevertheless help us to understand—a plot that places Anne Elliot in a series of relationships which draw out her dignity and measure that of others in relation to it. The plot moves Anne from Kellynch-hall, to Uppercross, to Lyme, to Bath, and at each place we meet one, two or more new characters who show us always a little more of the true dignity of Anne Elliot.

The first character we meet in *Persuasion* is Sir Walter Elliot. Suitably, he is introduced reading "the book of books" (7), which is not to be confused with the Holy Scriptures.

> Sir Walter Elliot, of Kellynch-hall, in Somersetshire, was a man who, for his own amusement, never took up any book but the Baronetage; there he found occupation for an idle hour, and consolation in a distressed one; there his faculties were roused into admiration and respect, by contemplating the limited remnant of the earliest patents; there any unwelcome sensations, arising from domestic affairs, changed naturally into pity and contempt, as he turned over the almost endless creations of the last century—and there, if every other leaf were powerless, he could read his own history with an interest which never failed . . . (3).

That Sir Walter reads only one book indicates his intellectual range. That he does it for amusement suggests what he asks from life. That he takes to the Baronetage to escape the duties of "domestic affairs" and to avoid "unwelcome sensations" points to the quality of his courage in face of life's realities. The Baronetage shows Sir Walter what life owes him, not what he owes it. That encouraging kind of bookkeeping is irresistible to him even though it leads to moral bankruptcy. Jane Austen does Sir Walter to a turn as he sits to her in a moment of leisure. We see that the only things he cares for are "vanity of person and of situation":

> He considered the blessing of beauty as inferior only to the blessing

of a baronetcy; and the Sir Walter Elliot, who united these gifts, was the constant object of his warmest respect and devotion (4).

Sir Walter likes the blessings of rank and good looks because they confer privileges that come with birth and need not be merited. But Kellynch-hall gives him "unwelcome sensations." It has a dignity that requires exertion on Sir Walter's part. Kellynch-hall has a "character of hospitality and ancient dignity to support" (13), but Sir Walter is incapable of supporting it. Kellynch-hall represents what life asks of the baronet and his eldest daughter, Elizabeth, but neither can measure up to life's demands.[21] To save their ancient and respectable family seat, they are unwilling to sacrifice "any indulgence of taste or pride" (10). Father and daughter can do nothing but feel themselves "ill-used" (10).

Unable of themselves to find any way to save Kellynch, they turn to Lady Russell for advice. On consultation with Anne, Lady Russell "drew up plans of economy."

> "If we can persuade your father to all this," said Lady Russell, looking over her paper, "much may be done. If he will adopt these regulations, in seven years he will be clear; and I hope we may be able to convince him and Elizabeth, that Kellynch-hall has a respectability in itself, which cannot be affected by these reductions; and that the true dignity of Sir Walter Elliot will be very far from lessened, in the eyes of sensible people, by his acting like a man of principle" (12).

The proposal is rejected out of hand. What Lady Russell proposes for the sake of "true dignity," Sir Walter finds "disgraceful":

> "What! Every comfort of life knocked off! Journeys, London, servants, horses, table,—contractions and restrictions everywhere. To live no longer with the decencies even of a private gentleman! No, he would sooner quit Kellynch-hall at once, than remain in it on such disgraceful terms" (13).

Sir Walter will quit Kellynch and move to Bath with Elizabeth where they "should lose neither consequence nor enjoyment" (14). He will rent the house to Admiral Croft:

> "I have let my house to Admiral Croft," would sound extremely well; very much better than to any mere *Mr.* — —; a *Mr.* (save, perhaps, some half dozen in the nation,) always needs a note of explanation. An admiral speaks his own consequence, and, at the same time, can never make a baronet look small (24).

The first three chapters of *Persuasion* show that Sir Walter and his daughter Elizabeth are without true dignity. They make the norm for dignity what they themselves have: rank and good looks. They live on what has come to them without any effort or merit on their part. They demand what they think due to them by their inherited position. If they cannot have consequence and amusement at Kellynch-Hall, they will have them at Bath. The Baronetage is truly their "book of books"; it is the bible of their lives. In it they find that heredity gives privilege. Kellynch-hall as "a house which had . . . a character of hospitality and ancient dignity to support" embarrasses Sir Walter and Elizabeth. Hospitality and ancient dignity imply something more than good looks and rank; they imply an obligation and a sense of duty that confers merit. Father and eldest daughter are adverse to obligation and unworthy of a respectable, hospitable, dignified home like Kellynch-hall. Anne Elliot, however, is equal to its demands.

Sir Walter thinks little of his daughter Anne. To him she was never good-looking; consequently, "he had never indulged much hope, he had now none, of ever reading her name in any other page of his favourite work" (6). By his standards, then, Anne is nothing: "she was only Anne" (5). But Anne is the image of her mother:

> Lady Elliot had been an excellent woman, sensible and amiable; whose judgment and conduct, if they might be pardoned the youthful infatuation which made her Lady Elliot, had never required indulgence afterwards (4).

When she was alive "method, moderation, and economy" prevailed at Kellynch-hall. Lady Elliot was equal to the demands of the inherent respectability and ancient dignity of her home. She responded to life and did not complain about being ill used. Characteristically, her daughter Anne makes the same kind of response to life when Kellynch is in danger:

> She considered it as an act of indispensable duty to clear away the claims of creditors, with all the expedition which the most comprehensive retrenchments could secure, and saw no dignity in anything short of it. She wanted it to be prescribed, and felt as a duty (12–13).

"Duty" is here seen as indispensable to "dignity" for Anne. Only by doing one's duty does one achieve true worth, true dignity. When she cannot convince her father of his duty to save Kellynch-hall, Anne at least tries to make Sir Walter realize the suitability of renting the house to Admiral Croft:

> "The navy, I think, who have done so much for us, have at least an equal claim with any other set of men, for all the comforts and all the privileges which any home can give. Sailors work hard enough for their comforts, we must all allow" (19).

But Sir Walter is not interested in people who merit what they get; he is only interested in the sound of "I have let my house to Admiral Croft." Anne is pleased that Kellynch-hall will give its comfort and hospitality to a man who has rendered his country service and merited them. When Anne later comes to know Admiral and Mrs. Croft, she feels "that they were gone who deserved not to stay, and that Kellynch-hall had passed into better hands than its owners' " (125).

Significantly, when the Crofts take over their new residence, they make some alterations in it. One is especially interesting:

> "I have done very little besides sending away some of the large looking-glasses from my dressing-room, which was your father's.

A very good man, and very much the gentleman I am sure—but I
should think, Miss Elliot" (looking with serious reflection) "I
should think he must be rather a dressy man for his time of life.—
Such a number of looking-glasses! oh Lord! there was no getting
away from oneself. So I got Sophy to lend me a hand, and we soon
shifted their quarters; and now I am quite snug, with my little
shaving glass in one corner, and another great thing I never go
near" (127–128).

Obviously, Jane Austen is having a great deal of fun here:
Admiral Croft talks about looking-glasses with "serious reflection"; the officer from Trafalgar feels threatened by a large
looking-glass that he never goes near. But insofar as all the glasses
make "getting away from oneself" impossible, they show us the
only side of Sir Walter Elliot we ever see—his egoism. When he
is unoccupied with "contemplating the limited remnant of the
earliest patents" and with polishing the Elliot entry in the
Baronetage to make it better reflect his family's present position,
he is occupied with looking at himself in the mirrors. Happily,
when Sir Walter moves from his ancestral house, the symbols of
rank and appearance, the Baronetage and the looking-glasses,
disappear from Kellynch-hall.

In this Elliots-of-Kellynch section of the novel the separation
of amusement and duty is brought continually to the fore. Their
final deflection is emphasized by Sir Walter and Elizabeth's going
off to Bath with Mrs. Clay—"I am sure Anne had better stay,
for nobody will want her in Bath" (33), says her sister—and
leaving Anne to see to things at Kellynch-hall. Anne tells Mary:

"I have been making a duplicate of the catalogue of my father's
books and pictures. I have been several times in the garden with
Mackenzie, trying to understand, and make him understand, which
of Elizabeth's plants are for Lady Russell. I have had all my own
little concerns to arrange—books and music to divide, and all my
trunks to repack, from not having understood in time what was
intended as to the waggons. And one thing I have had to do, Mary,

of a more trying nature; going to almost every house in the parish, as a sort of take-leave. I was told that they wished it'' (38–39).

To the very end of their residence there, Kellynch-hall makes too much of a call on duty and personal dignity for Sir Walter and Elizabeth. To the very end, consequence and amusement are sought as gratuities. To the very end, Anne is alone and committed at Kellynch-hall.

With the departure of the little group for Bath, Anne goes to help her sister Mary at Uppercross, ''glad to have any thing marked out as a duty'' (33). At Uppercross her attentions are divided between the cottage and the Great House. The confusion at Kellynch made demands on the Elliots to which Anne immediately responded, but no one seems much concerned by events at Uppercross Great House:

> to the Great House accordingly they went, to sit the full half hour in the old-fashioned square parlour, with a small carpet and shining floor, to which the present daughters of the house were gradually giving the proper air of confusion by a grand piano forte [sic] and a harp, flower-stands and little tables placed in every direction (40).

At Uppercross, as at Kellynch-hall, a way of life is changing, but there is no anxiety evident: ''Mr. and Mrs. Musgrove were a very good sort of people; friendly and hospitable, not much educated, and not at all elegant. Their children had more modern minds and manners'' (40). Henrietta and Louisa are responsible for the changes at the Great House, and the principle of change is clear: They ''were now, like thousands of other young ladies, living to be fashionable, happy, and merry'' (40). Anne enters into the life of Uppercross—both Great House and cottage—but she is necessarily alone. She is as much isolated among the Musgroves by her intelligence, elegance, and taste as she was among the Elliots at home.

Uppercross sustains in a new setting ''the plight of a sensitive woman in a society which has a measure for everything except sensitivity.''[22] Anne's change of residence again dramatizes her sense of duty and personal human dignity by giving her a chance to act selflessly. But before Anne is distinguished by her actions, she is revealed in depth by her thought:

> Anne always contemplated them [Henrietta and Louisa] as some of the happiest creatures of her acquaintance; but still, saved as we all are by some comfortable feeling of superiority from wishing for the possibility of exchange, she would not have given up her own more elegant and cultivated mind for all their enjoyments . . . (41).

Anne is irrevocably true to herself even though that truth is isolated from many enjoyments and forces upon her an awareness of "our own nothingness beyond our own circle" (42). Anne Elliot refuses to be anyone but herself, no matter what the cost.

Anne's stay at Uppercross cottage emphasizes her sense of herself and her expression of that self in activity. Life at Uppercross makes demands as life will anywhere, and Jane Austen is keen to show Anne's openness to life. Her readiness to meet the challenge of the cottage is carefully delineated in her attendance on her nephew after he has a "bad fall" (53) and the challenge of the Great House by her readiness to play the pianoforte while others dance.

Little Charles's bad fall puts his mother into a state of hysteria that renders her useless to her son:

> It was an afternoon of distress, and Anne had every thing to do at once—the apothecary to send for—the father to have pursued and informed—the mother to support and keep from hysterics—the servants to control—the youngest child to banish, and the poor suffering one to attend and soothe;—besides sending, as soon as she recollected it, proper notice to the other house, which brought her an accession rather of frightened, enquiring companions, than of very useful assistants (53).

As the boy mends, his mother feels ill-used by his convalescence

because she cannot dine out with her husband: "so, here he is
to go away and enjoy himself, and because I am the poor mother,
I am not to be allowed to stir . . ." (56). Anne sends Mary off
with Charles and sees to her nephew alone:

> They were gone, she hoped, to be happy, however oddly construc-
> ted such happiness might seem; as for herself, she was left with as
> many sensations of comfort, as were, perhaps, ever likely to be
> hers (58).

There is no reticence here on the narrator's part to make it clear
that those who have no claim on amusement are being amused,
while Anne is left to find another less amusing species of contentment:

> She knew herself to be of the first utility to the child; and what
> was it to her, if Frederick Wentworth were only half a mile
> distant, making himself agreeable to others (58).

What Anne is left to do is called by her brother-in-law "rather
hard" (58), and the evening away from the cottage proves rather
pleasant:

> Her brother and sister came back delighted with their new
> acquaintance, and their visit in general. There had been music,
> singing, talking, laughing, all that was most agreeable . . . (58).

A similar deflection of acceptance of duty from demand for
amusement is clear in Anne's services at the Great House. The
Musgrove "girls were wild for dancing; and the evenings ended,
occasionally, in an unpremeditated little ball" (47). Anne "played
country dances to them by the hour together" (47). This
might suggest a sense of family life for Anne, but it is really
evidence of less than that:

> The evening ended with dancing. On its being proposed, Anne
> offered her services, as usual, and though her eyes would sometimes
> fill with tears as she sat at the instrument, she was extremely glad

to be employed, and desired nothing in return but to be unobserved.

It was a merry, joyous party, and no one seemed in higher spirits than Captain Wentworth (71).

Jane Austen has driven an iron wedge between Anne's services and the others' amusement. When Wentworth later asks "whether Miss Elliot never danced?" the answer that is returned suggests more than a literal meaning for dancing. "Oh! no, never; she has quite given up dancing. She had rather play. She is never tired of playing" (72). Indeed, Anne's devotion to the pianoforte, like Jane Fairfax' in *Emma*, is a symbol of her elegance —of what the narrator calls "the nice tone of her mind" (28).

> She knew that when she played she was giving pleasure only to herself; but this was no new sensation: excepting one short period of her life, she had never, since the age of fourteen, never since the loss of her dear mother, known the happiness of being listened to, or encouraged by any just appreciation or real taste. In music she had been always used to feel alone in the world; and Mr. and Mrs. Musgrove's fond partiality for their own daughters' performance, and total indifference to any other person's, gave her much more pleasure for their sakes, than mortification for her own (47).

"In music she had been always used to feel alone in the world"— at Uppercross, as at Kellynch-hall, Anne is driven in upon herself and her own resources, for the tone of her mind is too finely pitched to be generally appreciated. Only Wentworth is capable of hearing it, but he as yet refuses to listen.

The gap between duty and amusement is further augmented in the series of events that begins with the walk to Winthrop and culminates in the trip to Lyme. Chapters 10 through 12 examine duty and amusement in relation to the central issue of persuasion, and at both Winthrop and Lyme accidents serve to focus the issue. Admiral Croft is not as good a horseman as he is a sailor. Wentworth ruminates:

"What glorious weather for the Admiral and my sister! They meant to take a long drive this morning; perhaps we may hail them from some of these hills. They talked of coming into this side of the country. I wonder whereabouts they will upset to-day. Oh! it does happen very often, I assure you—but my sister makes nothing of it—she would as lieve be tossed out as not" (84).

Louisa is quick to reply:

"If I loved a man, as she loves the Admiral, I would be always with him, nothing should ever separate us, and I would rather be over-turned by him, than driven safely by anybody else."

It was spoken with enthusiasm.

"Had you?" cried he, catching the same tone; "I honour you!"

And there was silence between them for a little while (85).

Firmness is here clearly set in opposition to persuasion. Louisa's firmness is again dramatized when Mary tries to persuade the walking party to turn back from Winthrop without visiting the Hayters. Louisa is firm in her refusal to turn back. She sees to it that Henrietta be allowed to visit with Charles Hayter. She says to Captain Wentworth,

"What!—would I be turned back from doing a thing that I had determined to do, and that I knew to be right, by the airs and interference of such a person?—or, of any person I may say. No,— I have no idea of being so easily persuaded. When I have made up my mind, I have made it" (87).

Wentworth commends her, "If Louisa Musgrove would be beautiful and happy in her November of life, she will cherish all her present powers of mind" (88).

Louisa's devotion to firmness is again in evidence in the Lyme sequence. Louisa, "armed with the idea of merit in maintaining her own way, bore down all the wishes of her father and mother" for putting off the trip to Lyme till the summer (94). Louisa remains a determined young woman in Lyme also: "as they drew near the Cobb, there was such a general wish to walk along it once more, all were so inclined, and Louisa soon grew determined, that the difference of a quarter of an hour, it was found, would be no difference at all . . .'' (108–109). On the Upper Cobb itself, Louisa proves what she had said about the superiority of courting danger with a lover. She would rather jump to her Frederick than walk down the stairs with her friends. She jumps, Wentworth misses catching her, and she is "taken up lifeless" (109). Louisa's determination to be amused gives way to Wentworth's reflection on duty: "Oh God! that I had not given way to her at the fatal moment! Had I done as I ought! But so eager and so resolute! Dear, sweet Louisa!" (116). Louisa's determination to be amused also gives way to another catalogue of duties for Anne to accept:

> Anne, attending with all the strength and zeal, and thought, which instinct supplied, to Henrietta, still tried, at intervals, to suggest comfort to others, tried to quiet Mary, to animate Charles, to assuage the feelings of Captain Wentworth. Both seemed to look to her for directions (111).

The sequence of events on the Winthrop walk and the Lyme visit takes place in autumn. At Winthrop "the last smiles of the year [are] upon the tawny leaves and withered hedges" (84). It is a "season of peculiar and inexhaustible influence on the mind of taste and tenderness" (84). But it is also a season in which one finds "ploughs at work, and the fresh-made path spoke the farmer, countering the sweets of poetical despondence, and meaning to have spring again" (85). And Anne, who is also devoted to duty—who recommends the prose of the moralists to Captain Benwick as an anodyne to the poetical despondence of Byron—seems also to have a claim on spring when she comes to Lyme:

> She was looking remarkably well; her very regular, very pretty features, having the bloom and freshness of youth restored by the

fine wind which had been blowing on her complexion, and by the animation of eye which it had also produced (104).

Wentworth looks at Anne and reflects that "even I, at this moment, see something like Anne Elliot again" (104). Wentworth's feelings toward Anne change at Winthrop and Lyme. From the Frederick Wentworth who "had not forgiven Anne Elliot" and who found that "her power with him was gone for ever" (61), he becomes the enlightened Frederick Wentworth. He learns from Louisa that Anne had refused to marry Charles Musgrove and he learns from William Elliot that Anne is still to be considered a beautiful woman. Also, he becomes her friend again. At Winthrop he hands her into the Croft's carriage:

> It was a remainder of former sentiment; it was an impulse of pure, though unacknowledged friendship; it was a proof of his own warm and amiable heart, which she could not contemplate without emotions so compounded of pleasure and pain, that she knew not which prevailed (91).

After her solicitude for all at Lyme, he asks her advice on his plan for breaking the news of Louisa's fall to her parents:

> the remembrance of the appeal remained a pleasure to her—as a proof of friendship, and of deference for her judgment, a great pleasure; and when it became a sort of parting proof, its value did not lessen (117).

Lyme has changed Wentworth. The "universal felicity and firmness of character" he celebrated at Winthrop can no longer appear good without the "proportions and limits" that belong to all things (116). Louisa Musgrove's determination to be amused at the expense of his duty has affected Wentworth. When he lifts her unconscious body from the pavement of the Lower Cobb and says, "She is dead, she is dead," Wentworth is correct. As far as he is concerned Louisa is dead; she cannot hope to have his love. "All must linger and gaze on a first return to the sea," says the narrator (96). As we linger and gaze on the spectacle of the sea in *Persuasion*, we realize that Jane Austen uses it as a source of life as well as of death. As Louisa dies, Anne comes to life. The "bloom and freshness of youth" are restored by the sea wind. In *Persuasion* autumn becomes Keats's season of "mellow fruitfulness" for Anne at the same moment that it is Tennyson's season of "mouldering flowers" for Louisa.[23]

At Lyme a conjunction is made between the human and natural elements in the story too. There was no need for Jane Austen to choose Lyme as the place of the Musgrove excursion. But the sea and sailors go together; therefore, it is appropriate that Wentworth find Anne most beautiful and dutiful by the sea. It is also appropriate that the sea serve to conjoin the end of one romance and the reawakening of another; that it serve to bring about "a proof of friendship" between Anne and Wentworth. It is fitting too that Lyme should witness the washing away of Wentworth's artificial and adamantine devotion to firmness of character as expressed in simple willful determination at the same time that it opens him to Anne's natural tenderness and beauty. It may be no accident, therefore, that at Lyme a cliff is seen to crumble and an orchard to bloom:

> the woody varieties of the cheerful village of Up Lyme, and, above all, Pinny, with its green chasms between romantic rocks, where the scattered forest trees and orchards of luxuriant growth declare that many a generation must have passed away since the first partial falling of the cliff prepared the ground for such a state, where a scene so wonderful and so lovely is exhibited, as may more than equal any of the resembling scenes of the far-famed Isle of Wight: these places must be visited, and visited again, to make the worth of Lyme understood (95–96).

The novel moves from the natural setting that Lyme provides, and after a brief interlude at Kellynch-lodge, locates Anne in Bath, where duty means nothing in comparison to amusement and where personal dignity is sacrificed on principle to artificial social standards of value. In Bath it makes all the difference in the world whether one lives in a Camden-place or a Laura-place or in Westgate-buildings. To be the cousin of a Lady Dalrymple in Bath is to be a somebody—even if one is as big a fool as Sir Walter Elliot. Anne is ashamed of her father's babbling about "our cousins Lady Dalrymple and Miss Carteret" (148), and she objects to his abject subservience. She tells William Elliot:

> "I suppose (smiling) I have more pride than any of you; but I confess it does vex me, that we should be so solicitous to have the relationship acknowledged, which we may be very sure is a matter of perfect indifference to them."
>
> "Pardon me, my dear cousin, you are unjust to your own claims. In London, perhaps, in your present quiet style of living, it might be as you say; but in Bath, Sir Walter Elliot and his family will always be worth knowing, always acceptable as acquaintance."
>
> "Well," said Anne, "I certainly am proud, too proud to enjoy a welcome which depends so entirely upon place."
>
> "I love your indignation," said he; "it is very natural. But here you are in Bath, and the object is to be established here with all the credit and dignity which ought to belong to Sir Walter Elliot" (151).

But Anne's father has no true dignity and she knows it. Bath has simply brought out the worst in him and Elizabeth:

> Their acquaintance was exceedingly sought after. Every body was wanting to visit them. They had drawn back from many introductions, and still were perpetually having cards left by people of whom they knew nothing (137–138).

There can be no worse indictment of Bath society than that it waits upon Sir Walter and Elizabeth and that it thinks Lady Dalrymple "a charming woman" because she has "a smile and a civil answer for every body" (150). After Lyme, Bath is a mausoleum. And since the dead do not recognize the living, Anne is very much out of place: "She is nothing to me, compared with you," says Elizabeth to the sycophant, Mrs. Clay (145).

"Bath is the moral wilderness which tests and reveals essential worth," writes David Daiches.[24] That is why the kind of existence Bath supports draws out Anne's "natural indignation," as William Elliot indicates. Both the words "natural" and "indignation" are important because indignation points to a radical lack of dignity, merit, or worth in the code of Bath society; and indignation is Anne's natural response to such artificiality. This natural indignation isolates her from her family and its synthetic amusements. She is once again forced to find her contentment apart from them.

Mrs. Smith enters the story at this point. She calls upon Anne's sense of duty: she had "two strong claims on her attention, of past kindness and present suffering" (152). Mrs. Smith's circumstances are wretched; nevertheless, Mrs. Smith is not:

> A submissive spirit might be patient, a strong understanding would supply resolution, but here was something more; here was that elasticity of mind, that disposition to be comforted, that power of turning readily from evil to good, and of finding employment which carried her out of herself, which was from Nature alone. It was the choicest gift of Heaven; and Anne viewed her friend as one of those instances in which, by a merciful appointment, it seems designed to counterbalance almost every other want (154).

Mrs. Smith's resolution and good spirits in adversity give her a personal dignity that pleases Anne but puzzles her father:

> "A poor widow, barely able to live, between thirty and forty—a mere Mrs. Smith, an every day Mrs. Smith, of all people and all names in the world, to be the chosen friend of Miss Anne Elliot, and to be preferred by her, to her own family connections among the nobility of England and Ireland! Mrs. Smith, such a name!" (158)

Anne can be the upright and understanding friend even of a Mrs.

Smith. Sir Walter, minding his status, trips over her name. Anne would rather visit and comfort a poor widow than wait on and flatter a rich one. She goes to Mrs. Smith; her father to Lady Dalrymple.

Mrs. Smith, of course, gives the coup de grâce to William Elliot, a stroke of esthetic anguish to be sure. But one sees that Jane Austen cannot resist the demolition of façades. The pretentious self-seeking suit of Sir Walter's baronetcy and Anne's hand must be shown for what it is. As Joseph Sittler interestingly enough puts it, the real cat is let out of the phoney bag.[25] William Elliot's attention to the good and the consequence of the family name is unmasked: his dutiful concern is found to be dutiful self-interest. As the pattern of the plot begins to move toward the association of duty and reward, William Elliot's mock duty gets a mock reward in Mrs. Clay. Anne's true duty gets a true reward: "She had never considered herself as entitled to reward for not slighting an old friend like Mrs. Smith, but here was a reward indeed springing from it" (212). Anne who has done so much—at Kellynch-hall, at Uppercross cottage, at Uppercross Great House, at Lyme—and been so little rewarded now fares better. The merit of true dignity begins to reap the reward of the duty that distinguished it.

What is especially interesting to note is how intimately Anne's rewards are integrated with Jane Austen's favorite theme of love and friendship. The reward of dignity and duty cannot fittingly be frivolous; it must be personally meaningful to fit naturally into the novel. In Bath, where most people make demands on life and ask their due as Sir Walters and Lady Dalrymples, an Anne Elliot can be easily overlooked. Were it not for the few—of whom Mrs. Smith is one—who meet the demands of existence on them, Anne's personal worth would be as little noted in Bath as her piano playing was at the Great House. The very hard reality of *Persuasion* is that where Anne is due love and friendship, it is denied her. Her father and sister

could not be more willfully careless of her: "she was only Anne."
But Mrs. Smith responds to Anne as a friend after she tells Anne
that "there is so little friendship in the world!" (156) At the
end of the novel Anne has only a modest dowry of loved ones to
present to her husband: "She had but two friends to add to his
list, Lady Russell and Mrs. Smith" (251). She is mortified that
she has

> no family to receive and estimate him properly; nothing of respect-
> ability, of harmony, of good-will to offer in return for all the
> worth and all the prompt welcome which met her in his brothers
> and sisters . . . (251).

Anne's regret emphasizes the basis of a meaningful life in *Persuasion*. In the midst of an alien society, where one is alone and has
only oneself, one must be true to the nice tone of one's own
mind. There may be no great happiness in this kind of life, no
great amusement; but in it alone can one find the dignity of personal integrity. One may live this way for eight years or forever;
the final alienation of goodness is not unknown. Anne Elliot knows
this as well as she knows everything else in *Persuasion*. If Frederick
Wentworth does not marry her, no one will. She will remain the
rest of her life only Anne Elliot, dignified, dutiful, but alone. It
seems that Jane Austen wants her readers to feel how very personal true human dignity is: "she would not have given up her
own more elegant and cultivated mind for all their enjoyments."
Thus Anne Elliot is allowed her eight years of relative solitude.
But once we realize this, we must also realize that Jane Austen is
not writing domestic tragedy. Rather, she is writing comedy with
a strong moral bent. As Paul Zeitlow writes,

> The disparity between the phenomenal good luck of the characters
> of *Persuasion*—they seem almost to be protected by the gods—and
> what their destinies would be if events took their normal course,
> serves to emphasize them without actually bringing them about.
> Chance and fortuitous circumstance in *Persuasion* can be seen as

Jane Austen's means for creating tragic effect while preserving comic form.[26]

The fidelity of Anne Elliot to the demands of existence by her life of duty deserves a reward. The reward is not Frederic Wentworth's £25,000; William Elliot has as much. Anne's reward is Wentworth's recognition of her personal dignity. He sees it in Anne with little Charles at Uppercross cottage, in Anne at the piano in the Great House, in Anne with the fallen Louisa on the Lower Cobb at Lyme, in Anne in conversation with Captain Harville in Bath. And he sees it finally even in Anne's rejection of his first proposal when she says:

> "I have been thinking over the past, and trying impartially to judge of the right and wrong, I mean with regard to myself; and I must believe that I was right, much as I suffered from it, that I was perfectly right in being guided by the friend whom you will love better than you do now. To me, she was in the place of a parent. Do not mistake me, however. I am not saying that she did not err in her advice. It was, perhaps, one of those cases in which advice is good or bad only as the event decides; and for myself, I certainly never should, in any circumstance of tolerable similarity, give such advice. But I mean, that I was right in submitting to her, and that if I had done otherwise, I should have suffered more in continuing the engagement than I did even in giving it up, because I should have suffered in my conscience. I have now, as far as such a sentiment is allowable in human nature, nothing to reproach myself with; and if I mistake not, a strong sense of duty is no bad part of a woman's portion" (246).

From the moment at Winthrop when Wentworth had handed Anne into the Crofts's carriage, his friendship for her became worthy of remark. His response to Anne is continuous and grows until she is moved to think that "He must love her" (186). What is natural in the order of things moves from seed to harvest in *Persuasion*, and in the midst of the burgeoning Anne is seen to "leave things to take their course."

> [She] tried to dwell much on this argument of rational dependance [sic]
> —"Surely, if there be constant attachment on each side, our hearts
> must understand each other ere long. We are not boy and girl, to be
> captiously irritable, misled by every moment's inadvertence, and
> wantonly playing with our own happiness" (221).

This is a beautiful statement and one made with a calm and
dignified sense of nature, where "things . . . take their course."
Its maturity and the dignity of the principals moved by the
natural processes of a deepening affective life required Jane
Austen to rewrite the famous "cancelled chapter" of the novel.
The emotional response of Wentworth to Anne cannot suitably
be to her refusal to reclaim the lease on Kellynch-lodge, which
would indicate to Wentworth that Anne will not marry William
Elliot. Rather his response is to Anne as a woman—a woman made
beautiful by love and fidelity:

> "Oh!" cried Anne eagerly, "I hope I do justice to all that is felt by
> you [Captain Harville], and by those who resemble you. God
> forbid that I should undervalue the warm and faithful feelings of
> any of my fellow-creatures. I should deserve utter contempt if I
> dared to suppose that true attachment and constancy were known
> only by woman. No, I believe you capable of every thing great and
> good in your married lives. I believe you equal to every important
> exertion, and to every domestic forbearance, so long as—if I may
> be allowed the expression, so long as you have an object. I mean,
> while the woman you love lives, and lives for you. All the privilege
> I claim for my own sex (it is not a very enviable one, you need not
> covet it) is that of loving longest, when existence or when hope is
> gone" (235).

As deep calls to deep, Wentworth touches the depths sounded by
Anne's words. He responds in kind:

> "Unjust I may have been, weak and resentful I have been, but never
> inconstant. You alone have brought me to Bath. . . . Too good, too
> excellent creature! You do us justice indeed. You do believe that

there is true attachment and constancy among men. Believe it to be
most fervent, most undeviating in

F.W." (237).

Jane Austen first shows us the true dignity of that constancy in the
duty-filled life of Anne Elliot, alone in the world and responsive to
life's call. Then she shows us the dignity of that constancy as
friendship grows to love and Wentworth responds to the goodness and excellence of Anne.

> . . . It helps us to know that no matter how fearfully complex and
> precarious our world can be, evil is evil, and good is good; that
> Anne deserves her Wentworth and Wentworth deserves his
> Anne. . . .[27]

"People are not interesting in the incoherent babbling with
which the articulation of passion takes place," David Daiches
remarks.[28] We are mercifully spared this false romanticism in
Persuasion. The novel moves to its close by reminding us of the
ironic truth that set it in motion. Anne's sufferings come to her
because at one moment in her life two people loved her dearly
enough to want the best for her. Their notions of what that best
might be were irreconcilable. In the moment of doubt, Anne
followed the path of duty. On that path she met the hard reality
of true dignity. *Persuasion* is thus a love story in which rank, consequence, and sundry artificialities at first prosper but ultimately
suffer their just deserts and in which love and duty first suffer but
ultimately prosper as nature conducts mature lovers to the mellow fruitfulness of an autumn love. The harvest of that love
reaps the reconciliation of those who love Anne best. As anta-
gonists in a conflict for Anne, Wentworth and Lady Russell were
so much against each other only because they so much loved her.
Before the novel ends, these primary representatives of love and
friendship unite to make Anne's happiness even greater. The
last artificial barrier is removed, rank and consequence give way,
firmness and persuasion are reconciled, and duty makes its last

call on Anne, who brings her friend and her lover together so
that Captain Wentworth and Lady Russell finally find in each
other the true personal dignity they have already found in her.

If the form is as much of the essence of the subject as the idea,
then the errand of form in a novel is to express that subject.
The subject of each of Jane Austen's novels is the maturation of a
young woman in relation to a paradigm for personal development.
Invariably, the Austen heroine meets with events that demand in
her a development of intellectual awareness, emotional discrimination, and moral strength. The pattern of events evokes reactions
that dramatize the failures and the successes of the heroine on
her way to that more complete life that Jane Austen symbolizes
by marriage. The man whom she marries must win the heroine's
esteem, friendship, gratitude, affection, and love—not infrequently in that order. Marriage follows on mature love and posits
the assimilation of the couple into the society in which they must
make their new life together.

This paradigm for personal happiness suggests the tenor of the
Austen canon. It is not a measure of the artistic value of the
individual novel. Each of the novels has its own particular
form, which is more or less satisfactory according to the degree
that it satisfies its own inexorable demands. I have tried to deline-
ate those demands as I saw them and as they were suggested to
me by the problems raised by scholars and critics. The esthetic
demands of *Sense and Sensibility* and of *Persuasion* seem never to be
quite adequately satisfied, but the salient markers in the subtle
worlds of these novels direct our attention to the relation of
esteem to love in the one novel and of dignity to duty in the
other. At the same time that we realize that the novels remain
flawed, we also realize that the flaws direct us to pervasive
features of *Sense and Sensibility* and of *Persuasion* and help us to
distinguish between novels that are flawed and novels that fail.

The esthetic demands of *Pride and Prejudice* and *Mansfield Park* are seen as satisfied (save perhaps for the undramatized ending of the latter) if we are willing to see them in a new perspective. The four obstacles to marriage in *Pride and Prejudice* and the action of feeling-as-one-ought in *Mansfield Park* suggest themselves as primary principles of formal integration in these novels. If we give them their due, *Pride and Prejudice* must reassume its classic status and *Mansfield Park* must be seen as appreciably closer to such status than has generally been admitted. The esthetic demands of *Northanger Abbey* are only satisfied when the traditional view of the novel as primarily a parody is scrapped. As a novel of initiation in which Catherine Morland undergoes a *rite du passage* into love and social reality, *Northanger Abbey* makes a great deal of sense. When the Gothic villain is recognized as the proud, mercenary, and mendacious father of the groom, the novel is recognized as emphasizing the discrimination and judgment of the heroine more than the failure of artistic discrimination and judgment on the part of the author. Such emphasis on the heroine's judgment at odds with her imagination in *Northanger Abbey* suggests its relation to *Emma*. No matter how differently critics interpret it, they insist that *Emma* is a masterpiece. The crucial problem of criticism in *Emma* is invarably one of handling its complexities. My intent in dealing with action and symbol was to show a heroine weaned from a life of egoism to one of true gentility and to suggest that the form is so much of the essence of the subject in *Emma* that its slightest alteration would inevitably effect a different meaning.

As I indicated in the Preface, many of the critical problems that are associated with Jane Austen's novels develop because of the tension that exists between the demands of structural patterns and the demands of characters to be persons. The problems of Dick Musgrove and of Mrs. Smith in *Persuasion* are of this kind. Dick's unworthiness is a signal that the hero and heroine must be worthy, and Dick's failure to be dutiful suggests that

Anne and Wentworth must not fail. Dignity and duty are inevitable realities on the path that intelligent and loving people must take to personal happiness. They are part of a pattern of personal fulfillment. To make that fulfillment actual, in *Persuasion*, Jane Austen was forced to introduce Mrs. Smith's revelations into the novel. This is a happy accident for Anne and Wentworth, but an unhappy device of plot for the reader. The novel survives Mrs. Smith and Dick Musgrove, but their presence suggests that in *Persuasion* (as earlier in *Sense and Sensibility*) Jane Austen's art shows that the tension between the demands of person and the demands of pattern is not completely resolved. The resolution is more satisfactory in *Northanger Abbey*, although the development of character is relatively slight at the same time that the development of a pattern of action by way of repetition of similar incidents is pronounced. *Mansfield Park*, so subtle and so sensitive in so many ways, suffers slightly, too, from the number of moral and emotional forces that are marshalled against Fanny's determination to preserve the integrity of her moral, emotional, and intellectual life. In *Northanger Abbey* Jane Austen seems to show something of Fielding's emphasis on pattern; in *Mansfield Park* something of Richardson's on moral character. But in *Pride and Prejudice* and in *Emma* the demands of pattern and person are met with such structural balance and literary wit that they seem as near to perfection as the work of mortals can be. Truly, in these two novels, the form is never found on any errand of its own.

Notes

Chapter I

1. I obviously do not agree with Marvin Mudrick, who sees "the ironic contrast" of Gothic and bourgeois values as "*so overt and extensive* that the formal unity of the novel depends on the author's success in maintaining each one as a distinct, continuous, and self-consistent commentary on the other," *Jane Austen: Irony as Defense and Discovery* (Princeton, 1952), pp. 38ff., italics mine.

2. C. S. Emden, "*Northanger Abbey* Re-Dated?," in *Notes and Queries*, CXCV (1950), 407–410. For comments on both *Northanger Abbey* and Emden's theory see B. C. Southam, *Jane Austen's Literary Manuscripts* (London, 1964), pp. 60–62, and A. Walton Litz, *Jane Austen: A Study of Her Artistic Development* (New York, 1965), pp. 175ff.

3. Frank J. Kearful, "Satire and the Form of the Novel: the Problem of Aesthetic Unity in *Northanger Abbey*," *Journal of English Literary History* (hereinafter cited as *ELH*) XXXII (1965), 511–527. Kearful writes: "The most important—the most interesting—critical problem concerning *Northanger Abbey* is the question of its aesthetic unity. Generally critics are forced to conclude that while brilliant in many parts, the book as a whole lacks a sufficiently consistent technique or unified form to make it a coherent work of art," p. 511.

4. *The Novels of Jane Austen*, ed. R. W. Chapman (3rd ed.), Vol. V: *Northanger Abbey and Persuasion* (London, 1959), p. 141. All subsequent references to this text will appear in parentheses following quotations from it.

5. *Irony*, p. 39.

6. Ibid., p. 40.

7. *Jane Austen's Novels: A Study in Structure* (London, 1957), p. 96.

8. *Jane Austen's Novels: The Fabric of Dialogue* (Columbus, O. 1962), p. 87.

9. Mary Lascelles writes that "there is within Catherine herself an

167

instinct, as of a wise child, that prevents her from abandoning her mind altogether to the world of illusion, and acquiring a taste for its poisonous magic fruit," *Jane Austen and Her Art* (London, 1963), p. 63.

10. *Artistic Development*, p. 65.

11. "Critical Realism in *Northanger Abbey*" in *Jane Austen: A Collection of Critical Essays*, ed. Ian Watt (Englewood Cliffs, New Jersey, 1963), p. 58.

12. Ibid., 59.

13. The one major attempt to solve the problem is Frank J. Kearful's (see n. 3). In his essay, Kearful seeks "a consistent technique or unified form" for *Northanger Abbey* (511). He sees *Northanger Abbey* not as a "satiric exposé" of the Gothic novel, but as "a positive novelistic alternative" to it (519). But in offering her alternative, Jane Austen has created a new illusion of life—a novel, one of "those illusions by which we master illusion" (527). She forces us to realize this by the way she concludes *Northanger Abbey*: "The book ends by denying the autonomy of the illusion it has presented, as in a Prospero-like closing gesture the narrator disperses the creatures of her imagination and the world they inhabit" (526). Consequently, "*Northanger Abbey* is an illusion about illusion and delusion, a book about life not being a book about life" (520). "Austen is writing what is not simply a novel or a satire, a burlesque or a parody, a comedy or a tragedy [sic], a romance or an anti-romance. She is, rather, combining elements of all these in such a fashion as to make us aware of the paradoxical nature of all illusion—even those by which we master illusion" (527).

In other words, Kearful sees the unity of *Northanger Abbey* in Jane Austen's working out of her intention—of making "us aware of the paradoxical nature of all illusion"—in a variety of seemingly contradictory techniques. Now if one is not alienated by Kearful's use of paradox and pun in this essay, he will find in it a genuine attempt to find order in the novel. But while I admire the attempt, I do not agree with the conclusions. Jane Austen never pretends to be telling a true life-story. Her novel may be a simulacrum of reality, but she never intends it to be taken for reality itself. Her continual references to Catherine as heroine—even as "my heroine" (74)—should make this clear. Moreover, the last paragraph of *Northanger Abbey* does not unequivocally return the reader to his own real world, as Kearful argues. Rather it returns the reader to the world of fiction by way of a parody of Richardson's moralizing. A clandestine correspondence between Catherine and Henry begins the last chapter, and Mr. and Mrs. Morland wink at it. The terror and trepidation of the Clarissa–Lovelace correspondence is mocked. Also, General Tilney proves to be the same kind of authoritarian figure that one meets in Mr. Harlowe in *Clarissa*. His tyranny, dictated by avarice, forces Clarissa to disobey him. Parental tyranny and filial disobedience lead to tragedy in Richardson's novel. The opposite is true in Jane Austen's. Parental tyranny and filial disobedience (Henry refuses to give up Catherine) lead to happiness. *Northanger Abbey* is finally comic. Its ending seems to be a parody of the preface of *Clarissa*, which explains that the novel was written "to caution Parents against the undue exercise of their natural authority over their Children in the great article of Marriage." Jane Austen refuses to be quite as explicitly didactic when she laughingly concludes: "I leave it to be settled by whomsoever it may concern, whether the tendency of this work be altogether to recommend parental tyranny, or reward filial disobedience" (252).

14. "The only source of the true Ridiculous (as it appears to me) is affectation. But though it arises from one spring only, when we consider the infinite streams into which this one branches, we shall presently cease to admire at the copious field it affords to an observer. Now, affectation proceeds from one of these two causes, vanity or hypocrisy: for as vanity puts on affectating false characters, in order to purchase applause; so hypocrisy sets us on an endeavour to avoid censure, by concealing our vices under an appearance of their opposite virtues," "Author's Preface" to *Joseph Andrews*, ed. Martin C. Battestin (Cambridge, Mass., 1961), p. 11.

15. Ibid., pp. 89–91.

16. Ibid., pp. 94ff.

17. Ibid., p. 19.

18. Ibid., pp. 28ff.

19. Ibid., pp. 30ff.

20. Ibid., p. 28.

21. Ibid., p. 26.

22. Ibid., p. 46.

23. Ibid., p. 255.

24. *The Question of our Speech* (Boston, 1905), p. 10.
25. Ch. 20 in consecutive numbering, or Vol. II, Ch. V in two-volume editions.
26. *Joseph Andrews*, p. 108.
27. *The Novels of Jane Austen* (London, 1964), p. 11.
28. For a discussion of the titles "First Impressions" and *Pride and Prejudice*, see Shunji Ebiike, " 'Pride and Prejudice' and 'First Impressions,' " *Studies in English Literature* (English Number 1965), 31–46, published by The English Literary Society of Japan.

Chapter 2

1. *Literary Manuscripts*, p. 56.
2. "On *Sense and Sensibility*," *Jane Austen: A Collection*, p. 49.
3. *Artistic Development*, p. 82.
4. *Fabric of Dialogue*, p. 84.
5. *Irony*, p. 89.
6. *Jane Austen: A Collection*, p. 42.
7. *Artistic Development*, p. 73.
8. Ibid., p. 82.
9. Ibid., p. 76.
10. Quoted in *Jane Austen: A Collection*, pp. 43ff.
11. *Irony*, p. 90.
12. Ibid.
13. *Jane Austen's Novels*, p. 30.
14. Ibid., p. 92.
15. *The Works of Jane Austen*, ed. R. W. Chapman (1st ed.), Vol. VI: *Minor Works* (London, 1958), p. 76. All subsequent references to this text will appear in parentheses following quotations from it.
16. *Artistic Development*, p. 82.
17. Ibid, p. 81.
18. *Jane Austen: A Collection*, p. 47.
19. *Fabric of Dialogue*, p. 53.
20. *Jane Austen: A Collection*, p. 51

21. *The Novels of Jane Austen*, ed. R. W. Chapman (3rd ed.), Vol. I: *Sense and Sensibility* (London, 1960), p. 15. All subsequent references to this text will appear in parentheses following quotations from it.

22. "Egoism and Altruism in *Sense and Sensibility*" (diss., Catholic University of America, 1964). In his study Laurence Connoley devotes one chapter to "Reasonable Explanations," a second to "Reasonable Expectations," and a third to "Reasonable Exertion." I am indebted to him for my terminology in this sentence.

23. Marianne emphasizes sensibility in taste in a way that is not sanctioned by the standard reference on the subject in Jane Austen's day. Hugh Blair writes, "But although Taste be ultimately founded on sensibility, it must not be considered as instinctive sensibility alone. Reason and good sense, as I before hinted, have so extensive an influence on all the operations and decisions of Taste, that a thorough good Taste may well be considered as a power compounded of natural sensibility to beauty, and of improved understanding," *Lectures on Rhetoric and Belles Lettres* (London: 9th ed., 1803), Vol. I, p. 24.

24. *The Rambler*, no. 47.

25. Mudrick, p. 86.

26. "Egoism and Altruism," p. 44.

27. Ibid.

28. If we turn to Hugh Blair, we realize how egoistic Marianne's desire for sameness in taste is. Blair writes, "In general, we may observe, that in the powers and pleasures of Taste, there is a more remarkable inequality among men, than is usually found, in point of common sense, reason and judgment. The constitution of our nature in this, as in all other respects, discovers admirable wisdom," *Lectures on Rhetoric*, p. 21.

29. Elinor is following a course of conduct recommended by Johnson in *The Rambler*, no. 47: "It seems determined, by the general suffrage of mankind, that sorrow is to a certain point laudable, as the offspring of love, or at least pardonable as the effect of weakness; but that it ought not to be suffered to increase by indulgence, but must give way, after a stated time, to social duties, and the common avocations of life."

30. *Jane Austen: A Collection*, p. 49. Watt appends an interesting comment to the excerpt from *Sense and Sensibility*: "The joy was not less intense because Elinor remembered that ladies do not run, and that they always shut the door."

31. John Gay, "Fable III. The Baboon and the Poultry. To a Levee-hunter." The first six lines of the poem follow:

> We frequently misplace esteem
> By judging men by what they seem.
> To birth, wealth, power, we should allow
> Precedence, and our lowest bow:
> In that is due distinction shown;
> Esteem is Virtue's right alone.

32. *The Works of Richardson*, intro. by Leslie Stephen (London, 1884), Vol. XI, p. 438.

Chapter 3

1. "I have called Miss Austen's earliest work, *Pride and Prejudice*, her masterpiece; and though some of her votaries have preferred to it *Emma*, or, as did the Prince Regent, *Mansfield Park*, the suffrage of the general reader has always been strong for *Pride and Prejudice*," H. W. Garrod, "Jane Austen: A Depreciation" in *Discussions of Jane Austen*, ed. William Heath (Boston, 1961), p. 35.

2. "Trying to recover here, for recognition, the germ of my idea, I see that it must have consisted not at all in any conceit of a 'plot,' nefarious name, in any flash, upon the fancy of a set of relations, or in any one of those situations that, by a logic of their own, immediately fall, for the fabulist, into movement, into a march or a rush, a patter of quick steps; but altogether in the sense of a single character, the character and aspect of a particular engaging young woman, to which all the usual elements of a 'subject,' certainly of a setting, were to need to be super-added," *The Art of the Novel: Critical Prefaces* (New York, 1953), p. 42. James substituted the word "action" for the more nefarious "plot." For the more than nominal difference between "plot" and "action" as the terms achieve concrete realization in novels, see Joseph Wiesenfarth, "Henry James: Action and the Art of Life," *Four Quarters*, XV (1966), 18–26, an article which compares *The Portrait of a Lady* with *Pride and Prejudice*.

3. *Jane Austen and Her Art*, p. 163.

4. Ibid., p. 162.

5. *The Novels of Jane Austen*, ed. R. W. Chapman (3rd ed.), Vol. II: *Pride and Prejudice* (London, 1959), p. 12. All subsequent page references to this text will appear in parentheses following quotations from it.

6. "An Unfortunate Mother's Advice to Her Absent Daughters," reprinted in part in Appendix II of Frank W. Bradbrook, *Jane Austen and her Successors* (Cambridge, 1966), p. 152.

7. Reuben Brower, *The Fields of Light* (New York, 1962), p. 179.

8. Ibid., p. 180.

9. Ibid.

10. For sake of convenience I have given the chapter numbers from editions of *Pride and Prejudice* that are numbered consecutively and in parentheses the volume and chapter numbers of the standard three-volume edition.

11. I use the word *psychomachy* to describe, in relation to Elizabeth, a condition of mind and emotions that was well explained by an anonymous critic for the *North British Review*, LXXII (April 1870), 129–152. "Again, she contemplates virtues, not as fixed quantities, or as definable qualities, but as continual struggles and conquests, as progressive states of mind, advancing by repulsing their contraries, or losing ground by being overcome. Hence again the individual mind can only be represented by her as a battle-field where contending hosts are marshalled, and where victory inclines now to one side and now to another," quoted in Lionel Trilling, "Introduction," *Emma* (Cambridge, Mass., 1957), p. xxii.

12. The presence here of a value like justice raises a problem. Dorothy Van Ghent has written that the "general directions of reference taken by Jane Austen's language . . . are clearly materialistic" (*The English Novel: Form and Function* [New York, 1961], p. 110). When a rich man sees a marriageable daughter, Mrs. Van Ghent writes, there is "no doubt he will buy, that is to say, 'fall in love' " (p. 102). "Categories" such as " 'trade,' 'arithmetic,' 'money,' 'material possessions' . . . indicate that kind of language Jane Austen inherited from her culture and to which she was confined . . ." (p. 109). Elsewhere, Mrs. Van Ghent affirms that "the moral life . . . will be equated with delicacy and integrity of feeling" (p. 103). But it is a logical necessity that one

either eat his cake or have it: either one or the other, but not both. If Jane Austen's society allowed her a materialistic vocabulary only, then she could not express non-materialistic values like "delicacy and integrity of feeling" because she had no words to do so. Indeed, if "to fall in love" is no more than "to buy," one wonders how delicacy of feeling and integrity of moral life can be spoken of at all. There is no such dilemma if one discards the theory of "dead metaphor." Important and characteristic words like "ashamed," "think," "feeling," "prejudiced," "despicably," "prided," "discernment," "detained," "generous," "vanity," blameable," "humiliating," "just," "humiliation," "love" (all words taken from the two paragraphs quoted from p. 208) abound in *Pride and Prejudice*. These words suggest, as C. S. Lewis has written, that the "great abstract nouns of the classical English moralists are unblushingly and uncompromisingly used" by Jane Austen ("A Note on Jane Austen" in *Jane Austen: A Collection*, p. 28). And with the nouns there are verbs, adjectives, and adverbs to carry serious moral judgments. To remain alive, a theory of dead metaphor has to discount not only the literal meaning of these words and those like them but also the structure of a plot wherein the human development of the characters depends on a literal reading of the diction.

13. It seems hardly necessary to make such a bland statement of facts; however, Geoffrey Gorer proves that it is. He writes, "Elizabeth, in *Pride and Prejudice*, does, it is true, marry young Mr. Darcy, but has anybody, even the author, been convinced that she loved him, or that she entertained any feelings warmer than respect or gratitude? Surely her own remark, that she must date her affection 'from my first seeing his beautiful grounds at Pemberley' (ch. 59), represents the psychological truth" ("The Myth in Jane Austen" in *Five Approaches to Literary Criticism*, ed. Wilbur Scott [New York, 1962], p. 94).

14. Lady Sarah Pennington in Bradbrook, 151ff.

15. This episode of Lydia's elopement with Wickham has not been to the liking of many critics. Brower, Mudrick, and Liddell, for instance, feel a drop in Jane Austen's imaginative power, a loss of irony, and a lack of dramatic coordination in it. There is, however, a structural coordination with the plot, as I have shown in my text. Besides, three other points may be made in reference to irony. First, the episode is ironic in its own way· Wickham, who has been angling throughout the novel,

makes the poorest catch in Lydia. Also, Elizabeth now reacts to Wickham in a manner for which she once condemned Darcy for reacting to Wickham. Again, the money Darcy once refused Wickham is now given him. Perhaps the irony is more attenuated than, and functionally different from what, it was previously, but irony nevertheless does function in this episode.

Another point that I cannot admit is that irony is the norm in the novel. An episode does not really have to be ironic to justify its presence in *Pride and Prejudice*. But Mudrick seems to argue that it does (*Irony*, pp. 111–115). In this episode, for instance, he maintains that Elizabeth is inconsistent because she does not react ironically to Lydia's elopement. Lydia, he argues, as a simple character is incapable of free choice; therefore, she is not susceptible to Elizabeth's moral indignation. Besides, Elizabeth's conventional moral reaction is atypical of her. But one need accept neither of these premises when evaluating the elopement. Elizabeth reacts in a straightforward manner to the faults of her mother, her sisters, Lady Catherine, Bingley, and occasionally even of Collins (all simple characters in Mudrick's opinion), and this suggests responsibility on their part and consistency on Elizabeth's when she reacts to Lydia. The "fogbank of bourgeois morality" that Mudrick feels conceals Jane Austen seems rather to be an acceptance on her part of a principle that holds fornication to be wrong. The principle may be conventional, but that does not discredit it. Neither Jane Austen nor Elizabeth needs to invoke irony here to discriminate good from bad. "Critics have seen [irony]," writes Donald J. Greene, ". . . as the mechanism of a refusal to make moral judgments about the world or to become emotionally involved with it. . . . This seems to me a fundamentally mistaken line of approach to any supremely great artist like Jane Austen" ("Jane Austen and the Peerage" in *Jane Austen: A Collection* p. 164).

16. *The Rambler*, no. 39.

17. *The Rambler*, no. 18.

18. *The Rambler*, no. 156.

19. *North British Review*, LXXII (April 1870), quoted in Trilling, "Introduction," *Emma* (Cambridge, Mass., 1957), p. xxii.

20. A. Walton Litz, *Artistic Development*, p. 102. In a similar vein, Joseph M. Duffy remarks, "Her vision might almost be reduced to the

assertion that, in spite of all evidence to the contrary, the sublime, the miraculous, and the ever possible human achievement is the love of two people for each other and the proliferation of that love in the family" ("Moral Integrity in *Mansfield Park*," *ELH*, XXIII [1956], 82).

21. T. S. Eliot, "What is a Classic?" reprinted in *On Poetry and Poets* (New York, 1961), p. 63.

22. "A Note on Jane Austen" in *Jane Austen: A Collection*, p. 3. One ought certainly to add to Lewis' remarks those of Alan D. McKillop: ". . . The social comedy can never be separated from a basic system of moral judgments; the release of free and humorous criticism or irony, as it is now fashionable to call it, is never irresponsible though it may well be lighthearted; as an aspect of the art of the novelist it stands in vital relationship to a plot structure which embodies a social structure." (*Early Masters*, p. 96).

23. For Dorothy Van Ghent, see note 12 above. Schorer first proposed the theory of dead metaphor in an essay "Fiction and the 'Analogical Matrix'" (*Kenyon Review*, XI [1949], 541–560), in which he discussed *Persuasion*. More recently, he affirmed the applicability of his theory to *Pride and Prejudice*: see "Introduction," *Pride and Prejudice* (Cambridge, Mass., 1956), pp. xv–xvi.

Chapter 4

1. *Jane Austen: Facts and Problems* (Oxford, 1961), p. 194.

2. In *Irony*, Mudrick sees *Mansfield Park* as Jane Austen's refusal to view life ironically, as she did in her earlier novels. The world that *Mansfield Park* affirms is one which "the author intrudes into her world of irony, which she had engaged herself to affirm" (p. 180). In this novel "the individual faces, not a choice of action, but a choice of allegiance; the action of the novel is a collision of worlds" (p. 155). These worlds are "proletarian Portsmouth, fashionable London, and Mansfield Park" (p. 155). Fanny and Edmund retreat from life to the Park.

3. In *Artistic Development*, Litz finds that in "*Pride and Prejudice* the hero

and heroine seek to achieve freedom by asserting their human ideals within the stubborn forms of society. . . . In contrast, *Mansfield Park* offers the paradox that freedom can only come through constant self-limitation." Further, "Elizabeth and Darcy know that they are not free, but they manage to create the illusion of freedom. *Mansfield Park* exposes the dangers of that illusion" (pp. 128ff.).

4. In his essay "Mansfield Park," reprinted in *Jane Austen: A Collection*, pp. 124–140, Trilling concerns himself with the novel's "uncompromising honesty," its "Christian heroine," and its "effort to encompass the grace of uncertainty and difficulty." The emphasis on naked difficulty and uncertainty in the moral life as against "morality as achieved style" suggests the possibility of the deception of "mere style" in morality. "If we perceive this . . . we must say . . . that its irony is more profound than that of any of Jane Austen's other novels. It is irony directed against irony itself." Trilling's conclusion offers direct disagreement with Mudrick's.

5. ". . . The novel is one of the last works of conservative eighteenth-century social criticism written at a time when the social horrors which were to occupy later nineteenth-century novelists were already portending," writes Duffy in "Moral Integrity and Moral Analysis in *Mansfield Park*," *ELH*, XXIII (1956), 73.

6. In *The Fabric of Dialogue* Babb writes that *Mansfield Park* "seems to me to be concerned fundamentally with defining moral integrity, a subject it explores by contrasting the self-centered behaviour of all the characters with Fanny's unselfishness" (p. 147).

7. "The theme has to do with meddling, seeking to impose one's will on creatures entitled to wills of their own, treating other lives as though one's designs for them were their chief reason for being" (p. 55). "Robbing people of their choice lies at the heart of virtually every significant incident in the novel," according to Edwards, "The Difficult Beauty of *Mansfield Park*," *Nineteenth-Century Fiction* (*NCF*) XX (1965), 56.

Other interpretations and evaluations of *Mansfield Park*, I think, have been superseded by those quoted in nn. 3–7. For instance, Q. D. Leavis's "A Critical Theory of Jane Austen's Writings," *Scrutiny*, X (1941), 61–87, 114–142, 272–294, cannot stand up under the criticism of B. C. Southam in *Jane Austen's Literary Manuscripts*, pp. 136–148. Consequently, the more considered biographical suggestions of A. Walton Litz's chapter on *Mansfield Park* deserve more attention than Mrs. Leavis' remarks. The careful work of critics like Trilling, Babb, Litz, and Edwards provides an answer to Kingsley Amis' question, "What Became of Jane Austen?"—reprinted in *Jane Austen: A Collection*, pp. 141–144—and makes his evaluation of *Mansfield Park* as "an immoral book" embarrassing. What can be said of Amis is equally true of Reginald Farrer, an excerpt of whose *Quarterly Review* essay of 1917 is reprinted as "On *Mansfield Park*" in *Discussions of Jane Austen*, ed. William Heath (Boston, 1916), 85ff.

8. Alan D. McKillop writes that Jane Austen's "themes represent the exquisite distillation of the social comedy of the *Grandison* tradition combined with a serious though not tragic treatment of family relationships which derives from *Clarissa*" (*Early Masters*, p. 96); Frank W. Bradbrook remarks that "Jane Austen's admiration for Richardson's works is well known. All three writers [Austen, Johnson, Richardson] could claim, in Johnson's words, that they had 'enlarged the knowledge of human nature, and taught the passions to move at the command of virtue' " (*Predecessors*, p. 12).

9. James Edward Austen-Leigh writes, "Her knowledge of Richardson's works was such as no one is likely again to acquire, now that the multitude and the merits of our light literature have called off the attention of readers from that great master. Every circumstance narrated in Sir Charles Grandison, all that was ever said or done in the cedar parlour, was familiar to her; and the wedding days of Lady L. and Lady G. were as well remembered as if they had been living friends" (*Memoir of Jane Austen*, ed. R. W. Chapman [London, 1963], p. 89).

10. *The Works of Samuel Richardson*, intro. by Leslie Stephen (London, 1884); all quotations with volume and page references are from this edition, in which *Grandison* comprises volumes IX–XII.

11. One cannot help adverting to Kant when one reads about duty's directing inclination and about man's feeling as he ought. Philosopher Frederick Copleston, s.j. writes that for Kant "the integrated personality, in whom inclination and duty coincide, has achieved a higher level of moral development than the man in whom inclination and desire are at war with his sense of duty." Kant presents "the ideal of a completely virtuous man who has overcome and transformed all desires which conflict with duty," *A History of Philosophy: Kant* (New York,

1960), Vol. VI, Pt. 2, pp. 109ff. In *Mansfield Park*, as in Kant's moral philosophy, the emphasis is on man's being one, and in his wholeness being at peace with himself.

12. *The Novels of Jane Austen*, ed. R. W. Chapman (3rd ed.), Vol. III: *Mansfield Park* (London, 1960), p. 10. All subsequent references to this text will appear in parentheses following quotations from it.

13. Andrew Marvell, "To His Coy Mistress," lines 41–46.

14. For other analyses of the significance of the Sotherton excursion, see Duffy, op. cit., pp. 83–85; Edwards, op. cit., pp. 52–55; and Charles Murrah, "The Background of Mansfield Park," *From Jane Austen to Joseph Conrad*, ed. R. C. Rathburn and Martin Steinmann, Jr. (Minneapolis, 1958), pp. 23–24.

15. *Jane Austen: A Collection*, p. 132.

16. Ibid.

17. "Order" is of such importance in *Mansfield Park* that Joseph W. Donohue, Jr., has given a unique interpretation of Jane Austen's comment, "Now I will try to write something else, & it shall be a complete change of subject—ordination." Donohue writes, "The problem of a disordered society and the possibility of its being restored to order is, I propose, the kind of ordination with which Jane Austen tasks herself in *Mansfield Park*" (*ELH*, XXXII [1965], 170). David R. Carroll presents the more standard reading of "ordination": "The action of the novel depends upon Edmund's balancing the claims of his vocation against those of his infatuation for Mary Crawford; and Fanny waits passively in the wings until he discovers the incompatibility of these claims" (*Modern Philology* [*MP*] LXII [1965], 218).

18. A different analysis of Fanny's association with the East room, with special emphasis on the significance of the fire, is given by Reuben Brower, "Introduction," *Mansfield Park* (Cambridge, Mass., 1965), pp. xvi–xxii. See also: Sister M. Lucy Schneider, "The Little White Attic and the East Room: Their Function in *Mansfield Park*," *ELH*, LXIII (1966), 227–235.

19. It is well to remember that Julia later sees the light and repents. Joseph M. Duffy remarks of Jane Austen that "she always introduces sufficient qualifications to avoid a rigidly deterministic explanation of behavior, but the distinction may be so fine as to be nearly imperceptible," pp. 77ff.

20. "Pictur'd Morals" is a phrase that David Garrick applied to Hogarth's *A Harlot's Progress, A Rake's Progress, Marriage à la Mode,* and *Industry and Idleness*; see V. de S. Pinto, "William Hogarth" in *From Dryden to Johnson,* Vol. 4, *A Pelican Guide to English Literature,* ed. Boris Ford (Harmondsworth, Middlesex, 1957), p. 281.
21. *The Rambler,* no. 97.
22. V. de S. Pinto, p. 283.
23. *Jane Austen: A Collection,* p. 140.
24. William Butler Yeats, "A Prayer for My Daughter," lines 75ff.

Chapter 5

1. Lascelles, p. 175; see also n. 4 on same page. E. N. Hayes writes that "*Emma* is not a novel of plot. Rather, it is a novel of characterization, a novel of ironic similarities and contrasts of character." His failure to see the structure of *Emma* and its implications may account for his title: "*Emma*: A Dissenting Opinion," *NCF,* IV (1949), 16.
2. *The Art of the Novel, Critical Prefaces,* ed. Richard P. Blackmur (New York, 1953), p. 42.
3. Ibid., p. 48.
4. *The Rhetoric of Fiction* (Chicago, 1963), p. 265.
5. Ibid., p. 260.
6. *The Novels of Jane Austen,* ed. R. W. Chapman (3rd ed.), Vol. IV: *Emma* (London, 1960), p. 484; all subsequent references to this text will appear in parentheses following quotations from it.
7. G. B. Stern and Sheila Kaye-Smith, *Talking of Jane Austen* (London, 1943), p. 176.
8. H. W. Garrod: "I am a little sorry for both parties when Emma marries Mr. Knightley," "Jane Austen: A Depreciation" in *Discussions,* p. 38. Mark Schorer: "And how 'happy' is this marriage, with Knightley having to move into old Mr. Woodhouse's establishment? Isn't it all, perhaps, a little superficial—not the writing but the self-avowals of the characters? A little perfunctory, as comedy may be, telling us

thereby that this *is* comedy?" ("The Humiliation of Emma Woodhouse"
in *Jane Austen: A Collection*, p. 109). Edmund Wilson: "Emma, who was
relatively indifferent to men, was inclined to infatuations with women;
and what reason is there to believe that her marriage with Knightley
would prevent her from going on as she had done before: from dis-
covering a new young lady as appealing as Harriet Smith, dominating her
personality and situating her in a dream-world of Emma's own in which
Emma would be able to confer on her all kinds of imaginary benefits
but which would have no connection whatever with her condition or
her real possibilities? That would worry and exasperate Knightley and
be hard for him to do anything about. He would be lucky if he did not
presently find himself saddled, along with the other awkward features of
the arrangement, with one of Emma's young protégées as an actual
member of the household ("A Long Talk About Jane Austen" in
Jane Austen: A Collection, p. 39). It is interesting to note in passing that
Wilson disclaims for *Emma* "any specific Freudian formula." Some
readers, however, remain unconvinced.

9. *Irony*, p. 201.

10. Ibid., p. 206.

11. Ibid., p. 194, n. 4.

12. Ibid., p. 181.

13. Farrer goes on at some length to explain why *Emma* is not an easy
book to read: "Take it all in all, *Emma* is the very climax of Jane Austen's
work; and a real appreciation of *Emma* is the final test of citizenship in
her kingdom. For this is not an easy book to read; it should never be
the beginner's primer, nor be published without a prefatory synopsis.
Only when the story has been thoroughly assimilated, can the infinite
delights and subtleties of its workmanship begin to be appreciated, as
you realise the manifold complexity of the book's web, and find that
every sentence, almost every epithet, has its definite reference to
equally unemphasized points before and after in the development of the
plot. Thus it is that, while twelve readings of *Pride and Prejudice* give you
twelve periods of pleasure repeated, as many readings of *Emma* give you
that pleasure, not repeated only, but squared and squared again with
each perusal, till at every fresh reading you feel anew that you never
understood anything like the widening sum of its delights" ("On
Emma" in *Discussions*, p. 102).

14. "Introduction" to *Emma* (Cambridge, Mass., 1957), p. viii.

15. "Hers, indeed, is a more exacting, a loftier and a finer code than that of older novelists; it was based on a high conception of the intrinsic worth of personality. Every one of her novels is the history of a process of self-correction and self-education, with inner harmony, understanding, integrity, and self-approval as the goal" (Ernest A. Baker, *History of the English Novel: Edgeworth, Austen, Scott* [London, 1935], Vol. VI, p. 72).

16. A. Walton Litz has made the apt comment that "With *Emma* . . . Jane Austen has achieved such a fine consistency of form that any critical approach seems woefully self-limiting." He nevertheless recognizes that "of all Jane Austen's novels *Emma* yields least readily to generalized discussion" (*Artistic Development*, p. 143). The present analytic approach is one of many that have been offered. For instance, Litz himself writes, "The basic movement of *Emma* is from delusion to self-recognition, from illusion to reality. The three major stages in the drama, corresponding roughly to the novel's three volumes, concern Emma's 'blindness' to the real natures of Mr. Elton, Frank Churchill, and finally Mr. Knightley; but all these errors of judgment are functions of her fundamental lack of self-understanding" (op. cit., p. 133). Mark Schorer suggests that "from an architectural point of view, *Emma* seems to consist of four movements, or of four intermeshing blocks, each larger than the preceding. Emma is always the focus for us, but her own stature is altered as one block gives way to the next—that is, she bulks less large in the whole action of each as one follows upon another." The "blocks" are those of Harriet, the Eltons, Frank and Jane, and Mr. Knightley ("The Humiliation," in *Jane Austen: A Collection*, p. 101). G. Armour Craig proposes that "the ruling principle of every participant in Highbury society is the dramatic principle of imputing feelings to conduct, and Emma achieves self-control when she perceives the impossible position—the non-existent rank—into which her imputations and suspicions would lead her" ("Jane Austen's *Emma*: The Truths and Disguises of Human Disclosure," *In Defense of Reading*, ed. Reuben A. Brower and Richard Poirier [New York, 1963], p. 251).

17. According to Gilpin, a picturesque group was made up of three: "But with *three*, you are almost sure of a good group, except indeed they all stand in the same attitude, and at equal distances. They generally

however combine the most beautifully, when two are *united*, and the third a little removed" (*Observations on the Mountains and Lakes of Cumberland and Westmorland*, "Explanation of the Prints," quoted in Bradbrook, *Predecessors*, p. 62). It seems to me especially appropriate to call this group of Mr. Woodhouse, Emma, and Mr. Knightley "picturesque" if one conceives the drama of *Emma* as involved in moving Emma from her father's side to that of Mr. Knightley. Miss Woodhouse becomes Mrs. Knightley. Gilpin's two-one grouping applies at both the beginning and end of *Emma*.

18. Thomas More, *Utopia*, II, 16; trans. and ed. H. S. V. Ogden (New York, 1949), p. 82.

19. Jonathan Swift, *Tale of a Tub: With Other Early Works: 1696-1707*, ed. Herbert Davis (Oxford, 1957), p. 108.

20. "Madame Bovary, by Gustave Flaubert" in *Madame Bovary: Backgrounds and Sources: Essays in Criticism*, ed. Paul de Man (New York, 1965), p. 340.

21. *The Journals of Kierkegaard*, trans. and ed. Alexander Dru (New York, 1959), p. 243.

22. Edgar F. Shannon, Jr., singled out a tableau of Emma, Mr. Knightley, and Mr. Woodhouse around the tea-table at Hartfield and suggested the anagogic significance of its implied third appearance and its relation to the rhythmic structure of the novel. In his discussion of the last scene, Shannon makes this acute observation: "The third occurrence of this tableau . . . after Emma has achieved full awareness, is only implied. . . . The author avoids the ineptness of depicting his scene at the end of the book—as much as to say, 'Look, here we are again, back where we started from, but with what a change in Emma!' Yet she provides for the reader such a resolution of her work. . . . Tranquility has replaced the stress created by Emma's misguided opinions and willful behavior" (*Emma*: Character and Construction," *Publications of the Modern Language Association of America* [*PMLA*], LXXI [1956], 649).

Chapter 6

1. *Jane Austen's Letters to her sister Cassandra and others*, ed. R. W. Chapman (London, 1959), p. 344.
2. *The Novels of Jane Austen*, ed. R. W. Chapman (3rd ed.), Vol. V: *Northanger Abbey* and *Persuasion* (London, 1959), p. 199. All subsequent references to this text will appear in parentheses following quotations from it.
3. *The Novels of Jane Austen*, p. 119.
4. *Irony*, p. 222.
5. *Jane Austen: A Biography* (New York, 1949), p. 394.
6. *Jane Austen: The Six Novels* (London, 1965), p. 182.
7. *Jane Austen and Her Art*, p. 193.
8. Craik, p. 197.
9. Jenkins, p. 246.
10. "Mansfield Park" in *Jane Austen: A Collection*, p. 139.
11. Mudrick, p. 211.
12. Ibid., p. 213.
13. Liddell, p. 128.
14. Ibid.
15. "Structure and Idea in Jane Austen's 'Persuasion,'" *NCF*, VIII (1954), 274.
16. Blackie, *Self Culture*, quoted in *The Oxford English Dictionary* under *dignity*; date, 1874.
17. *Artistic Development*, p. 154.
18. Mudrick, p. 213.
19. "Luck and Fortuitous Circumstances in *Persuasion*: Two Interpretations," *ELH*, XXXII (1965), 193.
20. Mudrick, p. 240.
21. To W. A. Craik, Kellynch is "a frigid place," *Six Novels*, p. 190. But it seems hardly to be that when the narrator can refer explicitly to its "character of hospitality and ancient dignity."
22. Mudrick, p. 239.
23. In "To Autumn" Keats writes of a "Season of mists and mellow fruitfulness" (v. 1). In "Song" ("A spirit haunts the year's last hours") Tennyson writes of "mouldering flowers" (v. 8). Keats sees autumn as a

season of ripeness; Tennyson sees autumn as a season of death and decay.

24. "Introduction" to *Persuasion* (New York, 1958), p. vii.

25. Sittler writes, "This amazing spinster is an instance of the fundamentally ethical nature of the craft of the artist. The task of the artist, as artist, is not to declare directly the Gospel of God; it is rather to speak the truth about the life of man, to let real cats out of phoney bags" (*The Structure of Christian Ethics* [Baton Rouge, Louisiana, 1958], pp. 20ff.).

26. Zeitlow, p. 195.

27. Ibid.

28. "Introduction" to *Persuasion*, p. xvi.

INDEX

Austen, Jane, concern for words, 28; influence of Fielding on, ix–xi, 3–9, 16, 20; influence of Richardson on, ix–xi, 59, 87–90, 102–03, 166, 169 *n* 13, 178 *nn* 8, 9; person *v.* pattern, structural demands of, viii, 165–66; position on marriage, 59, 76–7, 80, 83, 137; use of irony, 63, 65, 84–5, 103–04, 132, 142, 163, 174–75 *n* 15, 177 *n* 4

Babb, Howard, on *Mansfield Park*, 86, 177 *n* 6; on *Northanger Abbey*, 2–3; on *Sense and Sensibility*, 30, 34, 35
Blair, Hugh, on Taste, 171 *nn* 23, 28
Booth, Wayne, comparison of Jane Austen to Henry James, 109; on *Emma*, 110
Brower, Reuben, on *Pride and Prejudice*, 61

Carroll, David R., on *Mansfield Park*, 179 *n* 17
Chapman, R. W., on *Mansfield Park*, 86
Connoley, Laurence, on *Sense and Sensibility*, 48
Craig, G. Armour, on *Emma*, 182 *n* 16
Craik, W. A., on *Persuasion*, 140

Daiches, David, on *Persuasion*, 163
Donohue, Joseph W., Jr., on *Mansfield Park*, 179 *n* 17
Duffy, Joseph, on *Mansfield Park*, 86; on *Persuasion*, 142

Edwards, Thomas, on *Mansfield Park*, 86
Emma, bride as status, 133, 136; bride as symbol, 126–27; change in Emma, 133–34; concern for words in, 28; delimited world as symbol, 110; gentility, 133–37; irony, 132; masterpiece, 165; marriage as symbol, 110, 115; measurement of Harriet as symbol, 129; Mr. Knightley as voice of reality, 115, 116, 118–19, 121, 122, 128; Mr. Woodhouse as comic masterpiece, 113–14; person *v.* pattern, 166; pianoforte as symbol, 124–25, 127, 132, 135; portrait of Harriet as symbol, 118–19, 121, 129, 132; rhythm of action, 109; similarity to Henry James, 109; tableau, 112–13, 138, 183 *n* 22

Farrer, Reginald, on *Emma*, 111, 181 *n* 13
Fielding, Henry, emphasis on pattern, 166; formative influence on Jane Austen's fiction, ix–xi; *Joseph Andrews* and *Northanger Abbey*, 3–9; *Joseph Andrews*, the "Unfortunate Jilt" in relation to *Northanger Abbey*, 4–8, 16, 20
Form, errand of, viii, 164–66

Gay, John, on esteem, 58
Greene, Donald, on irony, 175 *n* 15
Gorer, Geoffrey, viii; on *Pride and Prejudice*, 174 *n* 13
Gothic novels, parody on, 1–3, 26–7

Hayes, E. N., on *Emma*, 180 *n* 1
Hogarth, William, in relation to *Mansfield Park*, 107

James, Henry, on form, viii; on plot, 172 *n* 2; on speech, 10
Jenkins, Elizabeth, on *Persuasion*, 140
Johnson, Samuel, on esteem, 58; on marriage, 76, 77, 80; on sorrow, 37, 40–1, 171 *n* 29

Kearful, Frank J., on *Northanger Abbey*, 167 *n* 3, 168–69 *n* 13
Kierkegaard, Soren, on imagination, 137

Lascelles, Mary, on *Northanger Abbey*, 167–68 *n* 9; on *Pride and Prejudice*, 60–1; on *Persuasion*, 140
Lewis, C. S., on irony, 84–5
Liddell, Robert, on *Northanger Abbey*, 26; on *Persuasion*, 140, 141–42
Litz, A. Walton, on *Emma*, 182 *n* 16; on *Northanger Abbey*, 3; on *Persuasion*, 142; on *Pride and Prejudice* in contrast to *Mansfield Park*, 176–77 *n* 3; on *Sense and Sensibility*, 30–1, 34

"Love and Freindship," treatment of sensibility in, 31; relationship to *Sense and Sensibility*, 31–4

Mansfield Park, concern for words in, 28; education 86, 90–2, 95, 99, 105–06; feeling as one ought, 90–1, 106; freedom *v.* responsibility, 90, 95; Hogarthian elements, 107; in relation to *Clarissa*, 103; in relation to *Pamela*, 87; in relation to *Sir Charles Grandison*, 87–90, 102–03; integrity, 86, 90–1, 99; integrity determined by education, 86, 106; integrity threatened, 96–8, 107; irony, 103–04, 177 *n* 4; love *v.* esteem, 96; order in, 179 *n* 17; person *v.* pattern, 166; place as extension of person, 91, 93, 103–04; principle of formal integration, 165; wilderness metaphor, 93–4

McKillop, Alan D., on Catherine Morland, 3; on irony, 176 *n* 22

Mudrick, Marvin, on *Emma*, 110–11; on *Mansfield Park*, 86, 176 *n* 1; on *Northanger Abbey*, 2, 167 *n* 1; on *Persuasion*, 140, 141, 143; on *Pride and Prejudice*, 175 *n* 15; on *Sense and Sensibility*, 30

Northanger Abbey, drama of word *v.* deed, 14; Gothic novel, 1–3, 25, 26; illusion in, 168–69 *n* 13; initiation novel, 165; parody of *Clarissa* in, 169 *n* 13; parody of Gothic novels, 1–3, 4–7, 26, 27; person *v.* pattern, 166; precision of language, 10–15; relation to *Joseph Andrews*, 3–9; problem of unity, 1–3, 26–7; unity through speech, 10; values, 9, 28; word-reality-judgment pattern, 22–5; words, Henry's use of, 10–15, Catherine's use of, 13, 14, 15–16, Isabella's use of, 13, 14, 16–18, 19, 28, John's use of, 18–19, 20–1, 28, Gen. Tilney's use of, 23–4, 28; words, relation of to reality, 9–22, 28; word play, 14–15

Pennington, Lady Sarah, on conduct, 60–1, 71

Persuasion, autumn, 154, 156, 163; Baronetage as symbol, 144; critical problems of Mrs. Smith and Dick Musgrove, 139–44; concern for words in, 28; dignity, 143, 157, 163; dignity and duty, relationship between, 142–43, 147; dignity and duty rewarded, 159–

61; dignity and "natural indignation," 158; dignity of Kellynch-hall, 145, 146, 149; duty, Anne's sense of, 147, 149–52, 154, 158, 163; duty *v.* amusement, 148, 151–53, 154, 155, 156–57; firmness *v.* persuasion, 153–54; flawed novel, 164; irony, 142, 163; lookingglass as symbol, 148; person *v.* pattern, 165–66; the sea, 155–56

Pride and Prejudice, appearance *v.* truth, 70; concern for words in, 28; coordination of physical event and spiritual experience, 82; courtship as ritual, 80; dramatic design, 63–5; esthetic fitness, 61, 82; four obstacles to marriage, 65–9, 78–80, 84; irony, 63, 65, 84–5; irony of Lydia's elopement, 174–75 *n* 15; marriage, 76–7, 80–1; mercantile metaphor, 85, 174 *n* 12; parallels, 72–4; person *v.* pattern, 166; picaresque background, 82; principle of formal integration, 165; values expressed by plot, 82–4

Radcliffe, Mrs. Ann, 9–10, 25, 26, 27; *Mysteries of Udolpho*, 21, 25

Richardson, Samuel, emphasis on moral character, 166; formative influence on Jane Austen's fiction, ix–xi, 178 *nn* 8, 9; *Clarissa*, in relation to *Mansfield Park*, 103, parodied in *Northanger Abbey*, 169 *n* 13; *Pamela* in relation to *Mansfield Park*, 87; *Sir Charles Grandison*, in relation to *Mansfield Park*, 87–90, 102–03, in relation to *Sense and Sensibility*, 59

Schorer, Mark, on *Emma*, 180 *n* 8, 182 *n* 16; on *Pride and Prejudice*, 85

Sense and Sensibility, concern for words in, 28; Eleanor as center, 51–2; esteem *v.* love, 28, 36, 43, 56–9; flawed novel, 164; "Love and Freindship," relationship to, 31–4; mysteries, 35–41, 44, 55–6; mystery of Edward Ferrars, 35–7; mystery of Brandon, 38–9; mystery of Willoughby, 40–1; parallels, 42–5; problem of Brandon's letter, 30, 59; revelation and crisis, 41–4; selfishness *v.* selflessness, 44–7, 49; sensibility, characteristics and caricature, 33–4; sensibility *v.* sense, 47–50, 53–5, 56; structural development, 25

Shannon, Edgar F., Jr., on *Emma*, 183 *n* 22

Southam, B. C., on *Sense and Sensibility*, 30

Stern, G. B., on *Emma*, 110

Swift, Jonathan, on imagination, 129

Trilling, Lionel, on *Emma*, 111; on *Mansfield Park*, 86, 97–8, 107, 177 *n* 4; on *Persuasion*, 140–41

Van Ghent, Dorothy, on *Pride and Prejudice*, 85, 173 *n* 12

Watt, Ian, on *Sense and Sensibility*, 30, 34, 35

Wilson, Edmund, on *Emma*, 181 *n* 8

Wright, Andrew, on *Northanger Abbey*, 2; on *Sense and Sensibility*, 31

Zeitlow, Paul, on *Persuasion*, 143, 160–61